# TEACH YOURSELF

## Shirley Baldwin
## and Sarah Boas

# Hodder & Stoughton

A MEMBER OF THE HODDER HEADLINE GROUP

# ACKNOWLEDGEMENTS

The authors and publishers are grateful to the following for supplying photographs or illustrations:

Adams Picture Library; J. Allan Cash Ltd; B. Furst; Vincent Martinelli; Spectrum Colour Library; Tony Stone Worldwide.

Long-renowned as the authoritative source for self-guided learning – with more than 30 million copies sold worldwide – the *Teach Yourself* series includes over 200 titles in the fields of languages, crafts, hobbies, sports, and other leisure activities.

*British Library Cataloguing in Publication Data*
Baldwin, Shirley
  Holiday Italian
  I. Title II. Boas, Sarah
  458.3421
ISBN 0 340 63120 1

First published 1988 as *Italian in a week*
Re-published 1995 as *Teach Yourself Holiday Italian*

| Impression number | 10 | 9 | 8 | 7 | 6 | 5 | 4 | 3 | 2 | 1 |
|---|---|---|---|---|---|---|---|---|---|---|
| Year | | 1999 | 1998 | 1997 | 1996 | 1995 | | | | |

Copyright © 1988; 1995 Shirley Baldwin & Sarah Boas

All rights reserved. No part of this publication may be reproduced or transmitted in any form or by any means, electronic or mechanical, including photocopy, recording, or any information storage and retrieval system, without permission in writing from the publisher or under licence from the Copyright Licensing Agency Limited. Further details of such licences (for reprographic reproduction) may be obtained from the Copyright Licensing Agency Limited, of 90 Tottenham Court Road, London W1P 9HE.

Typeset by Transet Ltd, Coventry, Warwickshire.
Printed in Great Britain by Butler & Tanner Ltd, Frome and London, for Hodder & Stoughton Educational, a division of Hodder Headline Plc, 338 Euston Road, London NW1 3BH.

# CONTENTS

# INTRODUCTION

**Holiday Italian** is a short course which will equip you to deal with everyday situations when you visit Italy: shopping, eating out, asking for directions, changing money, using the telephone and so on.

The course is divided into 7 units, each corresponding to a day in the life of Marisa Cole (English teacher) and Paul Henderson (fashion buyer) during their week in Italy. Each unit begins with a dialogue, which introduces the essential language items in context. Key phrases are highlighted in the dialogues, and the phrasebook section which follows lists these and other useful phrases and tells you what they are in English.

Within these units there are also short information sections in English on the topics covered, sections giving basic grammatical explanations, and a number of follow-up activities designed to be useful as well as fun. Answers can be checked in a key at the back of the book. English–Italian vocabulary is listed under topic headings on pp. 78–82, followed by an Italian-English vocabulary list.

## Pronunciation

1  Each part of every word is sounded. Consonants are mostly similar to English ones but vowels are 'purer', more like those of Scotland than southern England.
2  One part of every word is stressed more than the others. Usually this is the syllable before the last: c**o**me, andi**a**mo. Some words, however, are stressed on the last vowel, and when this happens the vowel always carries a written accent: caff**è**, cos**ì**. Many words have an irregular stress and these just have to be learnt as you go along: c**o**stano (and all 3rd person plurals), des**i**dera, s**u**bito, etc.

### Vowels

**a**  (i)  like *u* in *crust*:  b**a**nca
   (ii)  like *a* in *car*:  c**a**sa
**e**  (i)  like *ai* in *chair*:  c**e**ntro
   (ii)  like *e* in *peck*:  **e**cco

**i**  like *i* in *machine*:  vic**i**no
**o**  like *o* in *rope*:  s**o**le
   (ii)  like *o* in *not*:  n**o**tte
**u**  like *oo* in *moon*:  **u**na

**Consonants:** *Mostly similar to English but with the following exceptions:*

**c**  (i)  before **e, i** like *ch* in *chin*:  **c**entro
   (ii)  elsewhere like *c* in *cat*:  **c**omprare
**ch**  like *k* in *kilo*:  **ch**iamo
**g**  (i)  before **e, i** like *j* in *jam*:  **g**iorno
   (ii)  elsewhere like *g* in *got*:  pre**g**o
**gh**  like *g* in *got*:  tra**gh**etto
**gl**  like *ll* in *million*:  bi**gl**ietto
**gn**  like *ni* in *onion*:  ba**gn**o

**h**  never pronounced
**r**  or **rr**, always rolled:  se**r**a
**s**  (i)  like *s* in *sun*:  que**s**ta
   (ii)  like *z* in *zoo*:  compre**s**o
**sc**  (i)  before **e, i** like *sh* in *shin*:  pe**sc**e
   (ii)  elsewhere like *sk* in *skin*:  pe**sc**are
**z**  (i)  like *ts* in *rats*:  gra**z**ie
   (ii)  like *dz* in *adze*:  me**zz**o

# 1 ARRIVING IN ITALY

## INTRODUCING YOURSELF

When arriving at a port or airport you will find customs and passport procedures standard and easy to follow, as much information is given in English as well as Italian. Look out for these signs: **DOGANA** (Customs) and **CONTROLLO PASSAPORTI** (Passport Control).

### come si chiama?/what's your name?

Paul Henderson (38), a fashion buyer, is on a trip to Florence to buy clothes and accessories for his London shop. He arrives at Pisa airport where he has arranged to be met by Raffaella Festoso (32), a designer for an Italian fashion house.

| | |
|---|---|
| Raffaella: | **Buongiorno. Come si chiama, per favore?** |
| Paul: | **Io sono** Paul Henderson. E **lei, come si chiama**, signora? |
| Raffaella: | **Mi chiamo** Raffaella Festoso. **Piacere.** |
| Paul: | **Molto lieto**, signora. |
| Raffaella: | La mia macchina è qui vicino. Andiamo a Firenze? |
| Paul: | Benissimo, andiamo. |

# 1 ARRIVING IN ITALY

Arriving on the same plane is Marisa Cole (22), a teacher who has come to Italy to see her boyfriend Giancarlo (27) and to apply for a teaching job. It is Giancarlo's father Enrico, and mother Anna, who come to meet her.

Anna: **Buongiorno, scusi, lei è la signorina Cole?**

Marisa: Sì, sono Marisa Cole. Lei è la signora Lazzarini?

Anna: Sì, sono la madre di Giancarlo. **Le presento mio marito**, Enrico.

Enrico: Ben arrivata, signorina! Ha fatto buon viaggio?

Marisa: Sì, ottimo, grazie.

Anna: Marisa, dov'è il suo bagaglio?

Marisa: È proprio qui.

Anna: Enrico, **per piacere**, prendi la valigia e andiamo a casa.

(Enrico picks up Marisa's case)

Marisa: **Grazie**.

Enrico: **Prego**, signorina. Andiamo. È ora di pranzo.

**Saying hello and goodbye**    Note that **Buongiorno**, **Buonasera** and **Ciao** can be used when saying *Hello* or *Goodbye*. With friends, relatives or children, you can use **Ciao**.

| | |
|---|---|
| **Buongiorno** | Hello/good morning/good afternoon |
| **Buonasera** | Hello/good afternoon/good evening |
| **Buonanotte** | Good night |
| **Arrivederci** | Goodbye (informal) |
| **Arrivederìa** | Goodbye (formal) |

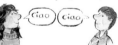

| | | |
|---|---|---|
| **Ciao, Giulia** | Hello, Julia | |
| **Ciao, Marco** | 'Bye, Mark | |

You should address a man as **signore**, a woman as **signora** and a girl or young unmarried woman as **signorina**. These titles are used much more frequently on their own than, for example, sir or madam are in English.

| | |
|---|---|
| **Buongiorno, signore*** | Good morning (to a man) |
| **Buonasera, signora** | Good evening (to a woman) |
| **Buonanotte, signorina** | Good night (to a young woman or girl) |

* **Signore** becomes **signor** in front of a name: **il signor Bianchini**. When addressing a man and a woman together you say **signori**.

*Greetings and introductions*

| | |
|---|---|
| (Lei) è il signor …? | Are you Mr …? |
| (Io) sono … | I am … |
| **Come si chiama?** | What's your name? (formal)/What's his, her name? |

# 1 ARRIVING IN ITALY

| | |
|---|---|
| Come ti chiami? | What's your name? (familiar) |
| Mi chiamo . . . | My name is . . . |
| Piacere (di conoscerla) | How do you do? |
| Piacere/molto piacere/molto lieto | Nice to meet you |
| Piacere mio | My pleasure |
| Le presento mia moglie/mio marito | This is my wife/my husband |
| Ben arrivato!Ben arrivata! | Welcome! |

## Words of courtesy

| | |
|---|---|
| Per favore/per piacere | Please |
| Grazie | Thank you |
| Grazie tante/grazie mille | Thank you very much |
| Prego | You're welcome |
| Non c'è di che | Don't mention it |
| Scusi | Excuse me |
| Molto gentile | It's very kind of you |

## Yes and no

| | | | |
|---|---|---|---|
| Sì/No | Yes/no | Sì, grazie/No | Yes, please/No, |
| Non è . . . | It's not | grazie | thank you |

## USEFUL WORDS AND PHRASES (DIALOGUE 1)

| | | | |
|---|---|---|---|
| la mia macchina | my car | Benissimo! | fine, excellent |
| è qui vicino | is quite near | Andiamo a Firenze | Let's go to Florence |

## USEFUL WORDS AND PHRASES (DIALOGUE 2)

| | |
|---|---|
| il padre di/la madre di | the father of/the mother of |
| Ha fatto buon viaggio? | Have you had a good journey? |
| Ottimo! | Great! |
| Dov'è . . .? | Where is . . .? |
| il suo bagaglio | your luggage |
| è proprio qui | it's right here |
| prendi la sua valigia | take her case |
| Andiamo a casa | Let's go home |

Enrico
il padre

Anna
la madre

Giancarlo
Il figlio

Margherita
la figlia

# 1 ARRIVING IN ITALY

## the way it works
### People and things

In Italian, words for people and things are either masculine or feminine. The word for *the* is normally **il** for a masculine noun — **il passaporto**   passport — and **la** for a feminine noun — **la valigia**   suitcase.

When a noun begins with a vowel, however, you use **l'** (**l'albergo** hotel), and with a masculine noun that begins with **z** or **s** + **consonant** you use **lo** (**lo zucchero**   sugar). Most nouns ending in **-o** are masculine and most nouns ending in **-a** are feminine. To make a noun plural **-o** changes to **-i** and **-a** changes to **-e**. The word for *the* also changes:

|  | singular | plural |  | singular | plural |
|---|---|---|---|---|---|
| *masc.* | **il** passaport**o** | **i** passaport**i** | *fem.* | **la** valig**ia** | **le** valig**ie** |

Some nouns end in **-e** in the singular. Some of these are masculine (**il padre, il piacere**) and others are feminine (**la madre, la notte**   night). All these nouns change the **-e** to **-i** in the plural: **i padri, le madri, le notti**.

### I am, you are

**Io sono Paul Henderson**                    I am Paul Henderson
**Lei è il signor Henderson**                  You are Mr Henderson
The most commonly used verb in Italian for 'to be' is **essere**.

| (io) sono | I am | (noi) siamo | we are |
|---|---|---|---|
| (tu) sei | you are (familiar) | (voi) siete | you are |
| (lei) è | you are (formal), she is | | |
| (lui) è | he is | (loro) sono | they are |

The words **io** (I), **tu** (you), **lei** (you, she), etc. are subject pronouns. They are not normally needed because the form and ending of the verb itself indicate who is the subject of the verb. They are, however, used when confusion might otherwise arise, or for emphasis.

Note that there are two words for 'you' in Italian. With people you don't know well use the formal **lei** form (sometimes written **Lei**). With everyone else (particularly with friends and relations) you can use **tu**. In the plural, the **voi** form can be used for everyone.

The **tu** form takes the second person of the verb, while the **lei** form takes the third person, just like *he/she*.

### Asking questions

There are various ways in which you can ask a question in Italian. For questions to which the answer is Yes or No you can use the same word order as a statement but with a questioning tone of voice.
Lei è il signor Henderson?                    Are you Mr Henderson?
Lei è la signora Lazzarini?                    Are you Mrs Lazzarini?

If you are almost sure the answer is Yes, you sometimes add **Vero?** or **No?** (aren't you?/Isn't it? etc.).

Other kinds of question start with words such as **Dove?** Where?:
Dov'è* il suo bagaglio?                        Where is your luggage?
*Note that **Dove** is shortened to **Dov'** before **è**.

# 1 ARRIVING IN ITALY

## Saying No

To make a negative statement just add **non** before the verb.

No, **non** sono il signor Henderson.    No, I'm not Mr Henderson.

## My, your, his/her (singular)

To say 'my' you use **il mio** before a masculine noun and **la mia** before a feminine noun. Note that the gender of these adjectives refers to the object possessed and not to the possessor. You omit the **il** or **la** when talking about a member of your family: **mio** marito, **mia** figlia. For a complete list of possessive adjectives, see p. 22.

| | | | |
|---|---|---|---|
| il mio bagaglio | my luggage | la mia valigia | my suitcase |
| il tuo bagaglio | your luggage (fam.) | la tua valigia | your suitcase (fam.) |
| il suo bagaglio | your luggage/ his/her luggage | la sua valigia | your suitcase (formal) his/her suitcase |

## things to do

1.1 **Buongiorno, signora**. Raffaella is meeting a lot of people today! How does she greet them all? Add **signore**, **signora**, or **signorina** when appropriate:

*In the morning:*
1 Mr Rinaldi (an elderly business colleague)
2 Mrs Marzella (a shopkeeper)
3 Claudia (her cousin)
*In the afternoon:*
4 Mr and Mrs Fallaci
5 Miss Giulia Neri (a friend of her mother)
6 Mauro (a friend from work)

1.2 **Come si chiama?** Practise the following mini-conversations:
1 Customs officer to Mr Jones:
   Customs officer:    Come si chiama?
   Henry Jones:        . . .
   He turns to Mrs Jones:
   Customs officer:    Lei è la signora Jones?
   Susan Jones         Sì, . . .
2 Radio interviewer talks to Patricia Fox and her young son, Ben:
   Interviewer:    Scusi, come si chiama, per favore?
   Patricia:       . . .
   Interviewer:    E suo figlio, come si chiama?
   Patricia:       . . .

1.3 Can you match the following questions and answers:
1 Come si chiama, per favore?    (a) Sì, sono la signora Bruni.
2 Lei è la signora Bruni?         (b) No, non sono il padre di Franco.
3 Dov'è il suo bagaglio?          (c) Mi chiamo Maria Roberti.
4 È la sua valigia?               (d) È proprio qui.
5 Lei è il padre di Franco?       (e) No, non è la mia.

# 1 ACCOMMODATION

## BOOKING A HOTEL ROOM

**Accommodation**    Hotels (**alberghi**) are classified into five categories
ranging from the De Luxe (**Categoria Lusso**) to the modest Class 1V.
Detailed lists of hotels, etc. can be obtained from the Italian National
Tourist Office (ENIT) or from the local **Azienda di Turismo** (Tourist Office).
Booking in advance is desirable, particularly in tourist areas and during
the high season.

Other forms of accommodation include boarding-houses (**pensioni** or
**locande**), farmhouses, mountain huts (**rifugi alpini**), villas and flats
(**appartamenti**), details of which can also be obtained from ENIT. There
are also about 50 youth hostels (**alberghi per la gioventù**) for YHA
members.

When you arrive you may have to fill out a registration form (**una scheda**)
giving details of nationality, address, occupation, passport number, etc.
Service (**il servizio**) and VAT (**IVA**) is usually included in the charge for
the room but breakfast is often not included. When paying the bill (**il
conto**) remember that you should obtain an official receipt for it.

# 1 ACCOMMODATION

## all'albergo/at the hotel

Raffaella takes Paul to his hotel to check in before she goes to her office.

Direttore:  Buonasera, signori, desiderano?
Paul:       **Ho prenotato una camera.**
Direttore:  Sì. Il suo nome, per favore.
Paul:       Henderson.
Direttore:  Bene. Un attimo, per favore. (checks
            his list) Henderson . . . Ah sì. **Camera
            singola con bagno, per tre notti.** Ecco
            la chiave, signore. Posso avere il suo
            passaporto, per favore?
Paul:       Sì, certo. (hands it over)
Direttore:  Grazie. (calls the lift boy) Mario, porta le valigie del signore al
            primo piano, camera numero quindici.
Paul:       **A che ora è la prima colazione?**
Direttore:  Dalle sette alle nove e mezzo.
Raffaella:  (to Paul) Tutto va bene? Allora io vado a casa, ma torno
            domani mattina alle dieci.
Paul:       Grazie mille, Raffaella. A domani.

## ha una camera?/do you have a room?

Back at home that evening, Raffaella wants to book a room in Verona for
Saturday. She is on the telephone to a hotel.

Raffaella:  **Vorrei prenotare una camera** per sabato. Ha **una doppia**, per
            favore?
Direttore:  Sì signora. Con bagno o con doccia?
Raffaella:  **Con bagno.**
Direttore:  Per quanto tempo?
Raffaella:  **Soltanto per una notte.**
Direttore:  Sì, ne abbiamo una, ... ma solo con
            doccia.

Raffaella:  **Va bene** con doccia. **Qual è il prezzo**
            della camera?
Direttore:  Novantamila lire per notte.
Raffaella:  **È compresa** la colazione?
Direttore:  No, la colazione è a parte, Sono quattromila lire in più.
Raffaella:  Beh ... **è un po' cara** ma ... Va bene, **la prendo.**

*USEFUL WORDS AND PHRASES*

| | |
|---|---|
| un attimo | one moment |
| sì, certo | yes, of course |
| torno domani mattina | I'll come back tomorrow morning |
| A domani! | Till tomorrow! |
| va bene | OK |
| benissimo | fine, excellent |
| Bè . . . | Well . . . . |

# 1  ACCOMMODATION

*Booking a hotel room*

| | |
|---|---|
| il direttore | manager |
| Desiderano? | Can I help you? What do you want? |
| Ha una camera? | Do you have a room? |
| Avete camere libere? | Do you have any vacancies? |
| Ho prenotato una camera | I have booked a room |
| Ho una prenotazione | I have a reservation |
| Il suo nome, per favore | Your name, please? |
| Vorrei prenotare una camera | I'd like to book a room |
| per sabato | for Saturday |
| . . . doppia/singola | . . . double/single |
| . . . con letto matrimoniale | . . . with a double bed |
| . . . con due letti | . . . with two beds |
| . . . con bagno/con doccia | . . . with bath/with shower |
| . . . senza bagno/solo con doccia | . . . without bath/with just a shower |
| . . . con balcone/con vista sul mare | . . . with a balcony/with a sea view |
| . . . sul davanti/. . . sul retro | . . . at the front/at the back |
| l'aria condizionata | air conditioning |
| il riscaldamento | heating |
| l'acqua calda/il gabinetto | hot water/lavatory |
| Per quanto tempo? | For how long? |
| Per una settimana/tre notti | For a week/three nights |
| Soltanto per una notte | One night only |
| Sì, ne abbiamo una | We have one |
| L'albergo è completo | The hotel is full |

(*For numbers see list on p. 78*)

> Spett Direzione
> Hotel Lungano
>
> Desidero passare una settimana a Firenze e vorrei
> sapere se avete disponibile una camera singola con
> bagno dal 22 settembre. In caso affermativo vi
> prego di comunicarmi il prezzo per la camera e
> colazione.
>
> In attesa della vostra conferma porgo
> Cordiali saluti
> Lesley Robertson

## Checking the price and what it includes

| | |
|---|---|
| Qual è il prezzo della camera? | What's the price of the room? |
| per la pensione completa | for full board |
| per mezza pensione | for half board |
| novantamila lire per notte | 90,000 lira per night |
| la colazione | breakfast |
| il servizio | service |
| È compresa la colazione? | Is breakfast included? |
| Prima colazione compresa | Breakfast included |
| Tutto compreso | Everything included |

# 1  ACCOMMODATION

| | |
|---|---|
| La colazione è a parte | Breakfast not included |
| in più | over and above |
| A che ora è la colazione? | What time is breakfast? |
| Dalle sette alle nove e mezzo | From 7 to 9.30 am |
| Posso vedere la camera? | Can I see the room? |
| È un po' (troppo) cara | It's too expensive |
| Non ha nulla di meno caro? | Have you nothing cheaper? |
| Va bene, la prendo | That's fine, I'll take it. |

### Keys, documents and luggage

| | |
|---|---|
| Qual è il numero della mia camera? | What's the number of my room? |
| Camera numero quindici | Room number 15 |
| Ecco la chiave | Here is the key |
| Per favore la chiave | The key, please |
| Posso avere il suo passaporto? | Please could I have your passport? |
| i documenti | the documents |
| la carta d'identità | identity card |
| Può compilare questa scheda? | Can you fill in this form? |
| il facchino | porter |
| Può far portare su i nostri bagagli? | Can you have our luggage sent up? |
| Porta le valigie | Carry the suitcases |
| al primo piano/al secondo piano | to the first floor/second floor |
| Avete il garage? | Do you have a garage? |
| Dove posso parcheggiare? | Where can I park? |

### The bill

| | |
|---|---|
| Partirò domani mattina | I'm leaving tomorrow morning |
| Mi faccia il conto, per favore | Could I have the bill please? |
| Ha fatto un errore nel conto, credo | I think there is a mistake in the bill |
| Accettate le carte di credito? | Do you accept credit-cards? |
| Tutto è compreso? | Is everything included? |

## BUYING A DRINK

**Italian bars**  As well as alcoholic drinks, bars and cafés serve coffee soft drinks and snacks. You sometimes have to pay for your drink beforehand at the cash-desk. After paying, you take your receipt (**lo scontrino**) to the counter and tell the barman what you want. You can then stand at the bar to have your drinks. If you want to sit at a table (**un tavolo**) and be served by a waiter (**un cameriere**) you pay afterwards and this is sometimes more expensive.

# 1 BAR AND SOCIAL

## che cosa prendi?/what'll you have?

Before supper Anna and Enrico take Marisa to a **caffè** where Giancarlo joins them.

Giancarlo:  **Ciao, Marisa, come stai?**
Marisa:  **Bene, grazie, e tu?**
Giancarlo:  **Così, così.** Hai fatto buon viaggio?
Marisa:  Sì, grazie.
(The waiter comes to take their order)
Giancarlo:  Cosa prendi?
Marisa:  **Un martini con ghiaccio per me.**
Giancarlo:  (turns to his parents) E per voi, mamma e papà?
Anna:  Per me un bicchiere di vino bianco.
Enrico:  **Io prendo una birra, grazie.**
Giancarlo:  (to waiter) Per la signorina un martini con ghiaccio, per la signora un bicchiere di vino bianco e per il signore una birra. E per me . . . un bitter, per favore.
Cameriere:  Benissimo, signori.
(He brings the drinks)
Giancarlo:  Grazie. Allora, **facciamo un brindisi! Cin-cin!**

*Here is a list of the drinks mentioned in the dialogue plus a few more . . . .*

| | |
|---|---|
| un caffè (espresso) | strong black coffee |
| un cappuccino | white frothy coffee |
| un caffelatte | ordinary white coffee |
| un caffè macchiato | with a dash of milk |
| un tè freddo | iced tea |
| un tè al latte | tea with milk |
| un tè al limone | tea with lemon |
| una coca-cola | coke |
| un'aranciata | orangeade |
| una limonata | lemonade |
| un succo di frutta | fruit-juice |
| di mela | apple-juice |

| | |
|---|---|
| una spremuta d'arancia | fresh orange-juice |
| di limone | fresh lemon-juice |
| un'acqua minerale | mineral water |
| un bicchiere di | a glass of |
| vino rosso | red wine |
| vino bianco | white wine |
| una birra (nazionale) | beer from Italy |
| un aperitivo della casa | nouse aperitif |
| una birra (estera) | foreign beer |
| un martini | martini |
| un vermut | vermouth |
| un bitter | type of aperitif |
| un americano | type of aperitif |
| un frullato | milkshake |

### Ordering drinks

| | |
|---|---|
| Cosa prendi?/Cosa prende? | What'll you have? |
| (Cosa) desiderano? | What would you like? |
| un martini con ghiaccio | a martini with ice |
| per me/per voi | for me/for you (plural) |

# 1 BAR AND SOCIAL

| | |
|---|---|
| un bicchiere di . . . | a glass of . . . |
| Io prendo . . . | I'll have |
| Mi dà . . . | Give me . . . |
| Ecco lo scontrino | Here's the receipt |
| Facciamo un brindisi! | Let's drink to our health! |
| Cin-cin! | Cheers! |

## the way it works

### Un/una

| | | | |
|---|---|---|---|
| **un albergo** | a hotel | **una camera** | a room |
| **un martini** | a martini | **una birra** | a beer |

The usual word for 'a' or 'an' in Italian is **un** for masculine nouns and **una** for feminine nouns.

However, with masculine words which begin with **s** + a second consonant, or with **z** or **ps** you say uno: **uno scontrino**  a receipt, **uno zucchino**  a courgette.

With feminine words which begin with a vowel you use **un'**: **un'aranciata**  an orangeade.

### Asking how someone is

| | |
|---|---|
| To ask how someone is, say: | Come sta? (formal) or |
| | Come stai? (familiar) |
| Answers might include: | Sto bene, grazie, e lei? (formal) or |
| | Bene, grazie, e tu? (familiar) |
| To which the first person | |
| might reply: | Bene, grazie. |
| Other phrases about one's | Così, così     So, so |
| state of health include: | Non c'è male     Not too bad |
| | Benissimo!     Fine! |

Note that **sto**, **stai**, **sta** are parts of the verb **stare** 'to be' which is mainly used to ask and describe how someone is, and in a few other idioms.

### Asking and telling the time (There is a list of numbers on p.78)

To ask the time, you say:  **Che ora è?** *or* **Che ore sono?**
To tell the time, you say:

| | |
|---|---|
| È l'una | (It's one o'clock) |
| È mezzogiorno | (It's midday) |
| Sono le tre | (It's three |
| | o'clock, etc.) |

meno un quarto          e un quarto

e mezzo

To say at what time something happens:
La colazione è **alle** otto.

. . . è **dalle** sette **alle** nove e mezzo.

Breakfast is at 8 o'clock.

. . . from 7 till 9.30.

# 1 BAR AND SOCIAL

## *Asking if something you want is available*

Look at the following phrases:

**Ha/Avete** una camera?　　　　　　Do you have a room?
Sì, ne **abbiamo** una　　　　　　　We have one.

These are parts of the useful verb **avere** (to have):

| | | | |
|---|---|---|---|
| **ho** | I have | **abbiamo** | we have |
| **hai** | you have (familiar) | **avete** | you have |
| **ha** | you have (formal) | | |
| **ha** | he/she/it has | **hanno** | they have |

## things to do

**1.4　Vorrei una camera**. You are a travel agent making a hotel booking for a party of people all of whom have different requirements . . . .

　1 one double room with bath　　4 one double room with twin beds

　2 one single room with bath　　　5 one single room with a sea view

　3 one single room with shower　　6 two single rooms with bath

**1.5　Che ore sono?** A passer-by asks you the time. But unfortunately each member of your family has a different time on his watch . . .
Sono le . . .

Someone's watch is rather slow　　and someone's watch must have stopped altogether!

**1.6　Desidera?** You have paid for your drinks and taken your **scontrino** to the **barista** (barman). This is what you want and you give him your order:
Mi dà . . .

12

# 2 FINDING YOUR WAY

## UNDERSTANDING DIRECTIONS

Breakfast (**la colazione**) is not considered a very important meal in Italy and most people just have coffee (**caffèlatte** is a mild black coffee with hot milk) with a bread roll (**un panino**) or a cake (**una pasta**).

## dov'è il duomo?/where is the cathedral?

Paul is having breakfast at his hotel. The waiter comes over to take his order.

Cameriere:  Prego, signore?
Paul:       Un caffèlatte e un panino, per favore.
Cameriere:  Subito, signore.

(After breakfast he goes to Reception to ask how to get to various places he wants to see)

Paul:       **Dov'è il Duomo, per favore?**
Direttore:  È in centro. Passi per il Ponte Vecchio e vada sempre dritto.
Paul:       **È lontano da qui?**
Direttore:  No, da qui sono dieci minuti a piedi.
Paul:       E dov'è la Galleria degli Uffizi?
Direttore:  Dopo il Ponte giri a destra. È proprio vicino.
Paul:       **Vorrei vedere** anche il Palazzo Vecchio.
Direttore:  Ah sì, è vicino alla Galleria degli Uffizi, in Piazza della Signoria.
Paul:       E **c'è una tabaccheria qui vicino?**
Direttore:  Sì . . ., ce n'è una in Via dei Velluti. Prenda la prima a sinistra poi la seconda a destra. È sulla destra a cento metri.

### Finding your way

| | |
|---|---|
| **Dov'è il duomo?** | Where is the cathedral? |
| **È in centro** | It's in the centre |
| **Passi per . . .** | Go along/across . . . |
| **il Ponte Vecchio** | The Old Bridge |

# 2 FINDING YOUR WAY

| | |
|---|---|
| vada sempre dritto | go straight ahead |
| È lontano da qui? | Is it far from here? |
| Abbastanza lontano | Quite a long way |
| è dieci minuti a piedi | ten minutes on foot |
| La Galleria degli Uffizi | The Uffizi Gallery |
| dopo il ponte giri a destra | after the bridge turn right |
| È proprio vicino | It's very near |
| È proprio vicino | It's very near |
| Vorrei vedere anche. . . | I'd also like to see . . . |
| Il Palazzo Vecchio | The Old Palace |
| vicino a . . . | near (to) . . . |
| Piazza della Signoria | Signoria Square |
| C'è una tabaccheria qui vicino? | Is there a tobacconist's near here? |
| Ce n'è una in Via dei Velluti | There's one in Via dei Velluti |
| prenda la prima a sinistra | take the first on the left |
| la seconda a destra | the second on the right |
| sulla destra/sulla sinistra | on the right/on the left |
| a due passi | two steps (very near) |

## TALKING ABOUT YOURSELF
### di dov'è?/where are you from?

Marisa is looking for a teaching job, and visits a language school.

Marco:     Buongiorno. **È americana?**
Marisa:    No, **sono inglese**. E lei, **di dov'è?**
Marco:     Sono italiano, **di Vicenza.** Di dov'è in Inghilterra?
Marisa:    **Sono di Londra.**
Marco:     Ah! Mi piace tanto Londra. Ma **parla molto bene l'italiano**.
Marisa:    Grazie. Mia nonna è italiana. Abita a Napoli. Senta, vorrei
           parlare con il direttore.
Marco:     Ha un appuntamento?
Marisa:    Sì, alle dieci e mezzo.
(At that moment the director comes in)
Direttore: Ah, buongiorno, s'accomodi,
           signorina. È americana?

### Nationalities and languages

| | |
|---|---|
| È americano?/americana? | Are you American? (male/female) |
| Sono inglese | I am English |
| Sono scozzese/gallese/irlandese | I'm Scottish/Welsh/Irish |
| Sono italiano/italiana | I am Italian (male/female) |
| mia nonna è italiana | my grandmother is Italian |
| di Vicenza/di Londra | from Vicenza/London |
| Abita a Napoli | She lives in Naples |
| Parla l'italiano | You speak Italian |
| Parla l'italiano?/l'inglese? | Do you speak Italian?/English? |
| Parlo tedesco/francese | I speak German/French |
| Capisce l'inglese? | Do you understand English? |

# 2 FINDING YOUR WAY

| | |
|---|---|
| **Capisco/Non capisco** | I understand/don't understand |
| **Capisco ma non parlo** | I understand but I don't speak |
| **più lentamente** | more slowly |
| **Ho capito** | I understand |

## USEFUL WORDS AND PHRASES

| | |
|---|---|
| **senta!** | listen! |
| **Vorrei parlare con . . .** | I'd like to speak to . . . |
| **Ha un appuntamento?** | Do you have an appointment? |
| **s'accomodi** | sit down, make yourself comfortable |

# the way it works

## Asking for and understanding directions

The easiest way of doing this is to say: **Dov'è . . .?**
Dov'è il duomo? Where is the cathedral?
You will probably hear some of the following instructions:

| | | | |
|---|---|---|---|
| vada . . . | go . . . | passi per . . . | go along . . . |
| prenda . . . | take . . . | giri . . . | turn . . . |

Listen in particular for the following phrases in reply:

| | |
|---|---|
| **a destra** | right |
| **sempre dritto** | straight ahead |
| **a sinistra** | left |

More specifically:

| | |
|---|---|
| la prima a destra | first street on the right |
| la seconda a sinistra | second street on the left |

And sometimes you will be told how far it is
and how long it will take you:

| | |
|---|---|
| È a due chilometri | It's two kilometres away |
| Sono cinque minuti | It's five minutes |

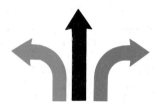

## There is/there are

In Italian you say simply: **C'è** (there is) or **Ci sono** (there are).

| | |
|---|---|
| **C'è** una banca | There is a bank |
| **Ci sono** tre camere | There are three rooms |

To say 'there is one (of them)' you insert **ne**:

| | |
|---|---|
| **Ce n'è** uno/**Ce ne sono** due | There is one/There are two of them |

Note that the question form is identical:
C'è una banca? Is there a bank?

## Some useful place words

| | | | |
|---|---|---|---|
| **accanto a** | beside | **in fondo** | at/to the end |
| **dopo** | after | **lì, qui** | there, here |
| **dietro** | behind | **fino a** | as far as, until |
| **davanti** | in front | **l'incrocio** | crossroads |
| **di fronte** | opposite | **il semaforo** | traffic-lights |
| **per** | along | **il ponte** | bridge |

15

# 2 FINDING YOUR WAY

## At/to/from/of/in/on

There are several examples of these useful words in this unit.

| | | | |
|---|---|---|---|
| **a** Napoli | at Naples | **a** destra | (to the) right |
| **di** Londra | from London | **da** qui | from here |
| **in** Piazza Santa Croce | in Santa Croce Square | | |

When used with the definite article (at the, from the, of the, etc.), these words combine with **il, lo, la, l', i, gli, le**:

| | |
|---|---|
| **alla** galleria **degli** Uffizi | to the Gallery of the Uffizi |
| La Piazza **della** Repubblica | the Square of the Republic |
| **sulla** destra | on the right-hand side |

Here is a table giving all the combined forms:

| | | il | lo | la | l' | i | gli | le |
|---|---|---|---|---|---|---|---|---|
| *to/at* | a | **al** | **allo** | **alla** | **all'** | **ai** | **agli** | **alle** |
| *by/from* | da | **dal** | **dallo** | **dalla** | **dall'** | **dai** | **dagli** | **dalle** |
| *of/from* | di | **del** | **dello** | **della** | **dell'** | **dei** | **degli** | **delle** |
| *in/into* | in | **nel** | **nello** | **nella** | **nell'** | **nei** | **negli** | **nelle** |
| *on* | su | **sul** | **sullo** | **sulla** | **sull'** | **sui** | **sugli** | **sulle** |

Note that **in** is used in several colloquial expressions without the definite article, to mean 'to' or 'in':

| | |
|---|---|
| Vado **in** albergo/**in** banca. | I'm going to the hotel/to the bank. |

## I'd like to . . .

Note the very useful expression **vorrei** which is used to mean 'I'd like . . .' and is followed by an infinitive (or dictionary form):

Vorrei vedere . . .   I'd like to see   Vorrei parlare . . .   I'd like to speak

**Vorrei** is part of the verb **volere** (to want). Here is the present tense:

| | | | |
|---|---|---|---|
| **voglio** | I want | **vogliamo** | we want |
| **vuoi** | you want (familiar) | **volete** | you want |
| **vuole** | he/she wants, you want | **vogliono** | they want |

## Saying where you come from

| | |
|---|---|
| If someone asks you: | Di dov'è (lei)? |
| you will be able to answer: | Sono di Manchester, Chicago, etc. |
| You might be asked: | È irlandese? |
| to which you can reply: | Sì, sono irlandese *or* |
| | No, sono americano. |

## Regular verbs group 1 (parlare)

**Parlare** is an example of an **-are** verb (named after its infinitive – or dictionary – ending) which is the first of four regular verb groups in Italian.

| | |
|---|---|
| **Parla** l'inglese? | Do you speak English? |
| **Parla** molto bene l'italiano | You speak Italian very well |

It is worth noting how the verb **parlare** (to speak) is formed:

| | | | |
|---|---|---|---|
| parl**o** | I speak | parl**iamo** | we speak |
| parl**i** | you speak (familiar) | parl**ate** | you speak |
| parl**a** | you speak, he/she speaks | parl**ano** | they speak |

# 2 FINDING YOUR WAY

## *things to do*

**2.1**  You want to visit the following places but you are not sure where they are. How do you ask?
1 Piazza della Repubblica
2 Palazzo Vecchio
3 Palazzo Pitti
4 l'Azienda di Turismo
5 La Posta

**2.2**  Look at the map of Florence (Firenze). You are standing (marked X) in the Via del Corso on the corner of the Via dei Calzaioli (the street of the shoemakers). Can you tell from the following instructions which of the places above you are being directed to?
1 Giri a sinistra e vada sempre dritto a Piazza della Signoria. È sulla sinistra, in fondo alla piazza. (*2*)
2 Giri a sinistra e prenda la seconda a destra. Vada fino al primo incrocio. È lì di fronte. (*5*)
3 Vada dritto fino al secondo incrocio. (*1*)
4 Passi per Piazza della Repubblica e vada sempre dritto. In Via dei Tornabuoni giri a destra. È sulla sinistra. (*4*)

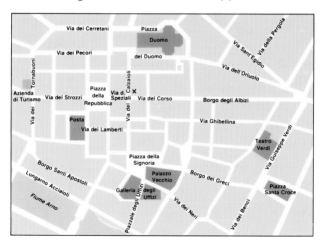

**2.3**  Can you match the following questions and answers?
1 Parla italiano?
2 Di dov'è?
3 C'è una toilette qui?
4 Dov'è il Palazzo?
5 Dove abita?

(a) A Londra.
(b) È in fondo alla Piazza.
(c) Capisco ma non parlo.
(d) Di Chicago.
(e) Sì, lì sulla sinistra.

# 2  SHOPPING, CLOTHES, ETC.

## BUYING A HANDBAG

## quanto costa?/how much is it?

Marisa decides to go and buy herself a handbag. She goes to a leather shop (**una pelletteria**) in Piazza Santa Croce.

Commessa:   Buongiorno, signorina. Desidera?
Marisa:     **Vorrei** una borsa di pelle.
Commessa:   Va bene. Di che colore?
Marisa:     Beh … nera o marrone.
Commessa:   S'accomodi, signorina. (She goes to fetch a selection) Le piace questa nera?
Marisa:     Sì **è bella ma è un po' grande.** (Sees one on a shelf behind the counter) Quella lì è più piccola, quella nera. **Mi fa vedere quella,** per favore?
Commessa:   Sì certo. (She gets it down) Eccola.
Marisa:     **È bellissima. Quanto costa?**
Commessa:   Questa? Costa duecentomila.
Marisa:     **È un po' cara.** Ma è bella e spaziosa.
Commessa:   E di ottima qualità, signorina.
Marisa:     **Mi piace molto** . . . Sì, **la prendo.**

# 2 SHOPPING, CLOTHES, ETC.

*Shopping – buying a handbag*

| | |
|---|---|
| una borsa di pelle | leather handbag |
| Di che colore? | What colour? |
| nero/a, marrone | black, brown |
| Le piace . . .? | Do you like . . .? |
| è bello/a | it's beautiful |
| un po' (troppo) grande | a bit too big |
| troppo piccolo/a | too small |
| non mi piace | I don't like |
| questo/a, quello/a | this (one), that (one) |
| più piccolo/a, più grande | smaller/larger |
| Mi fa vedere . . .? | Please could you show me . . .? |
| bellissimo/a | very beautiful |
| Costa duecentomila | It costs 97 000 lire |
| un po' caro/a | a bit expensive |
| spazioso/a | spacious |
| di ottima qualità | top quality |
| mi piace molto | I like it very much |
| Lo/la prendo, li/le prendo | I'll have it, I'll have them |
| Quanto costa?/Quanto costano? | How much does it/do they cost? |
| S'accomodi alla cassa | Please go to the cash-desk |
| Accettate carte di credito? | Do you accept credit-cards? |

## mi piace molto/I like it very much

Paul arrives at the Trade Fair with Raffaella to meet the directors of various Italian fashion houses. He stops at Moda Italiana.

Paul: (to the secretary) Buongiorno. Sono Paul Henderson, direttore della ditta inglese 'Fashion Link'. Ho un appuntamento con il suo direttore alle 15.00. Ecco il mio biglietto da visita.

Segretaria: Sì, un momento. Prego, signore, s'accomodi.

(They start looking around)

Raffaella: Questo vestito bianco e nero è molto bello. Le piace, Paul?

Paul: Sì è bello, ma **preferisco quello lì. Mi piacciono questi** pantaloni larghi e comodi.

Raffaella: Quella gonna a quadretti è molto stravagante!

Paul: **Non mi piace molto** quella giacca corta. È troppo stretta.

Raffaella: Ma guardi quel cappello giallo! Che colore!

Paul: D'accordo. Ah! Ecco il direttore.

(The director comes over to greet them)

Direttore: Buongiorno, signor Henderson. Le piacciono i miei modelli per l'estate?

# 2 SHOPPING, CLOTHES, ETC.

Paul:       Sì, certo. Per cominciare, può farmi un preventivo per questi
            vestiti bianchi di seta e per quelle gonne di cotone.
Direttore:  Benissimo! S'accomodi nel mio ufficio, signori.

### Buying clothes

| | |
|---|---|
| questo vestito bianco e nero | this black and white dress |
| molto bello | very pretty |
| preferisco | I prefer |
| quello lì | that one over there |
| questo qui | this one here |
| Mi piacciono | I like (plural) |
| questi pantaloni | these trousers |
| È/Sono troppo . . . | It is/They are too . . . |
| largo/larga/larghi/larghe | large, wide |
| lungo/lunga/lunghi/lunghe | long |
| comodo/a/i/e | comfortable |
| corto/a/i/e | short |
| stretto/a/i/e/ | narrow, tight |
| quella gonna | that skirt |
| a quadretti | checked, with checks |
| è molto stravagante | it is very odd |
| quella giacca | that jacket |
| Ma guardi quel cappello giallo! | But look at that yellow hat! |
| Di che colore? | What colour? |
| Che colore! | What a colour! |
| Non ha qualcosa … | Haven't you anything… |
| …di miglior qualità/di meno caro? | …better/cheaper? |
| No, grazie, è tutto | No thanks, that's all |

### Sizes

**Women's dresses**

| | | | | | | | |
|---|---|---|---|---|---|---|---|
| British | 8 | 10 | 12 | 14 | 16 | 18 | 20 |
| Continental | 36 | 38 | 40 | 42 | 44 | 46 | 48 |

**Shoes**

| | | | | | | | |
|---|---|---|---|---|---|---|---|
| British | 3 | 4 | 5 | 6 | 7 | 8 | 9 |
| Continental | 36 | 37 | 38 | 39–40 | 41 | 42 | 43 |

**Collar sizes**

| | | | | | | | |
|---|---|---|---|---|---|---|---|
| British | 14 | 14½ | 15 | 15½ | 16 | 16½ | 17 |
| Continental | 36 | 37 | 38 | 39–40 | 41 | 42 | 43 |

| | |
|---|---|
| Che numero? | What size (shoes)? |
| Che taglia? | What size (clothes)? |
| Taglia quarantadue | Size 42 |
| un paio di scarpe | a pair of shoes |
| Posso provarlo? | Can I try it on? |
| Come va?/Come vanno? | How does it/do they look? |
| Non va bene | It doesn't fit |
| Ha qualcosa . . .? | Do you have anything . . .? |
| . . . di più piccolo/grande | . . . bigger/smaller |

*(For colours and clothes items, see p. 79–80)*

# 2 SHOPPING, CLOTHES, ETC.

### Other useful phrases

| | |
|---|---|
| Ecco . . . | Here is . . . |
| il mio biglietto da visita | my business card |
| per cominciare | to start with |
| Può farmi un preventivo? | Can you give me an estimate? |
| di seta/di cotone | silk/cotton |

## the way it works

### I like it!

You say: **Mi piace** for 'I like . . .' (one thing) and **Mi piacciono** for 'I like . . .' (more than one).

| | |
|---|---|
| **Mi piace** questa camicia | I like this shirt |
| **Mi piacciono** questi maglioni | I like these sweaters |
| **Le piace** questa borsa? | Do you like this bag? |

### It's lovely!

Look at the following phrases from the dialogues:

| | |
|---|---|
| Quest**o** vestit**o** è molto bell**o**. | This dress is very nice. |
| (La bors**a**) è bell**a** e spazios**a**. | (The bag) is pretty and spacious. |

The ending of the adjective changes according to the gender of the noun it accompanies. Adjectives which end in **-o** in the masculine change to **-a** in the feminine; and to **-i** or **-e** in the plural:

| | |
|---|---|
| L**e** scarpe sono troppo strett**e**. | The shoes are too tight. |
| I sandal**i** sono molto comod**i**. | The sandals are very comfortable. |

Note that **molto** (very) and **troppo** (too much) do *not* change.

| | masc | fem | | masc | fem |
|---|---|---|---|---|---|
| *sing* | bell**o** | bell**a** | *sing* | piccol**o** | piccol**a** |
| *plural* | bell**i** | bell**e** | *plural* | piccol**i** | piccol**e** |

Adjectives which end in **-e** (masculine and feminine) change to **-i** in the plural:

| | |
|---|---|
| *sing*  grand**e**, ingles**e** | *plural*  grand**i**, ingles**i** |

**Note:** adjectives usually follow the noun. However, some common adjectives such as **bello** can precede the noun, in which case the forms of the adjective endings are similar to those of the definite article: un **bel** vestito, una **bella** gonna, un **bello** spezzato, un **bell**'abito.

### This and that, these and those

**Questo** means 'this' and 'this one' and **quello** means 'that' and 'that one'. Here are the endings for **questo**:

| | *this* | *these* |
|---|---|---|
| *masc* | questo modello, quest'anello | questi modelli |
| *fem* | questa borsa | queste borse |

**Quello** is more complicated, following the same rules as the definite article:

| | *that* | *those* |
|---|---|---|
| *masc* | quel modello | quei modelli |
| | quello zoccolo (*clog*) | quegli zoccoli (*clogs*) |
| | quell' albergo | quegli alberghi |
| *fem* | quella borsa | quelle borse |
| | quell' arancia | quelle arance |

# 2  SHOPPING, CLOTHES, ETC.

## Possessive adjectives

When followed by a plural noun, the possessive adjective also has a plural form.
**i miei** modelli                                    my models (*masc*)
**le mie** gonne                                      my skirts (*fem*)
Here is the complete list:

| singular | | plural | | |
|---|---|---|---|---|
| *masc* | *fem* | *masc* | *fem* | |
| mio | mia | miei | mie | *my* |
| tuo | tua | tuoi | tue | *your (fam.)* |
| suo | sua | suoi | sue | *his/her/its/your* |
| nostro | nostra | nostri | nostre | *our* |
| vostro | vostra | vostri | vostre | *your* |
| loro | loro | loro | loro | *their* |

## things to do

**2.4**  **Vorrei una borsa bianca.** Can you tell the assistant the colour you want?

**2.5**  **Mi piace quest'orologio. Quanto costa?**(I like this watch? How much is it?). You are buying presents and have seen certain things you like. But you need to know how much they all cost . . .

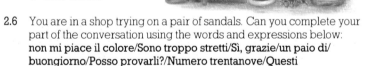

  1  un anello
  2  una bottiglia di profumo
  3  una spilla
  4  dele cinture

**2.6**  You are in a shop trying on a pair of sandals. Can you complete your part of the conversation using the words and expressions below:
**non mi piace il colore/Sono troppo stretti/Sì, grazie/un paio di/ buongiorno/Posso provarli?/Numero trentanove/Questi**

| | |
|---|---|
| Commessa: | Buongiorno. Cosa desidera? |
| You: | Buongiorno. Vorrei ................ sandali. |
| Commessa: | Che numero? |
| You: | ................ |
| Commessa: | (She shows you some blue ones) Le piacciono questi? |
| You: | Mi piace il modello ma ................ |
| Commessa: | Vediamo allora. Abbiamo questi sandali anche in nero. |
| You: | ................ |
| Commessa: | Certo. (you try them on) Le piacciono? |
| You: | Non vanno bene. ................ |
| Commessa: | Li abbiamo nel quarantuno. Vuole provarli? |
| You: | ................ |
| Commessa: | Come vanno? |
| You: | ................ sono un po' grandi! |
| Commessa: | Mi dispiace (*I'm sorry*) ma non li abbiamo nel quaranta. |
| You: | Grazie, ................ |

# SHOPPING, POSTCARDS AND STAMPS

## BUYING POSTCARDS, ETC.

**Il tabaccaio** (tobacconist) sells postage stamps (**francobolli**) as well as tobacco products (**sigarette** cigarettes), the sale of both items being state monopolies in Italy. Look for a large T-sign outside. Inside you will find that you can buy postcards (**cartoline**) and the necessary stamps to go with them, and perhaps have a drink as well, as the **tabaccheria** is often also a bar. A letter-box (**buca delle lettere**) may be red or yellow and is marked with the word **poste.**

## dal tabaccaio/at the tobacconist's

Paul's in the mood for writing postcards and goes into a **tabaccheria** with Raffaella. They look at the postcards together.

| | |
|---|---|
| Paul: | **Cos'è questo?** |
| Tabaccaio: | Questo è il Campanile. |
| Paul: | È molto bello. **Prendo questa**, e questa del Duomo . . . Vorrei anche una cartolina del Ponte Vecchio. Ah! Eccola. **Quanto costano le cartoline?** |
| Tabaccaio: | Duecento l'una. |

# 3 SHOPPING, FOOD

Paul: **Prendo** queste tre cartoline. **Vorrei anche tre francobolli** per la Gran Bretagna. **Quanto costa un francobollo** per una cartolina?

Tabaccaio: Seicento (600) lire, signore.

Paul: Allora, tre francobolli da seicento. **Quant'è in tutto?**

Tabaccaio: Sono seicento lire le cartoline e milleottocento (1800) lire i francobolli. Duemilaquattrocento (2400) lire in tutto.

Paul: Ecco duemilacinquecento lire.

Tabaccaio: Grazie. Cento di resto a lei.

### Talking shop

| | |
|---|---|
| **Cos'è questo?** | What's this? |
| **Questo è . . .** | It is/this is . . . |
| **Prendo questa** | I'll have this one |
| **Vorrei anche una cartolina** | and I'd like a postcard |
| **un francobollo per la Gran Bretagna** | a stamp for Great Britain |
| **tre francobolli da seicento** | three stamps at 600 lire |
| **ecco(lo), ecco(la)** | here (it) is |
| **Quanto costano . . .?** | How much are . . .? |
| **l'uno, l'una** | each (one) |
| **Quant'è (in tutto)?** | How much is it (altogether)? |
| **di resto a lei** | change for you |

## BUYING FOOD

Foodshops are generally open from about 8.30am until 7pm (or 8pm in the summer). However, they close for lunch between about 1pm and 3pm (or 4pm in the summer). You will find some open on Sundays and most shut for half a day some time during the week.

# 3 SHOPPING, FOOD

## vorrei un chilo di mele/I'd like a kilo of apples

Anna and Enrico have gone shopping to buy food for the family. First they go to the greengrocer's (**il fruttivendolo**).

| | |
|---|---|
| Negoziante: | Buongiorno, signora, desidera? |
| Anna: | **Vorrei un chilo di mele** rosse e **mezzo chilo di pere. Ha dell'uva bianca?** Ne vorrei un chilo e mezzo e due chili di pomodori maturi. |
| Negoziante: | Vuole altro? Basta così? Allora – mele, pere, uva, pomodori – quattromilacinquecento lire (L4.500) in tutto. |
| Anna: | Ecco a lei cinquemila lire (L5.000). |
| Negoziante: | Cinquecento (L500) di resto. Arrivederci e grazie. |

Next they go to the butcher's (**la macelleria**).

| | |
|---|---|
| Negoziante: | Prego, signora? |
| Anna: | Vorrei del maiale, per favore. |
| Negoziante: | Mi dispiace, signora, ma non ne abbiamo stamattina. Abbiamo vitello, manzo, agnello . . . |
| Anna: | Allora, **mi dà del vitello,** per favore? Lo vorrei tenero e magro. |
| Negoziante: | Ecco, signora. Quattro etti di carne buona. Altro? |
| Anna: | **No, basta così.** Grazie. |

Lastly they go to the grocer's (**alimentari**).

| | |
|---|---|
| Negoziante: | Cosa desidera, signora? |
| Anna: | **Ha del salame nostrano? Ne vorrei tre etti,** e poi due etti e mezzo di prosciutto crudo. |
| Negoziante: | **Va bene così?** Altro? |
| Anna: | Mi dà un po' di formaggio – del pecorino piccante, per favore. E vorrei anche dell'olio . . ., dello zucchero . . ., un litro di latte . . ., un chilo di caffè . . ., e sei uova. |
| Negoziante: | Ecco a lei, signora. Basta così? |
| Anna: | Sì, grazie. Quant'è? |
| Negoziante: | Allora sono . . . (adding up) undici e sei – undicimilaseicento lire in totale. |
| Anna: | Mi dà un sacchetto di plastica, per favore? |
| Negoziante: | Certo, signora. |

*What the shopkeeper might say*

| | |
|---|---|
| **Cosa desidera?/Desidera?/Prego?** | Can I help you?/What do you want? |
| **Vuole altro?/Altro?** | Anything else? |
| **Basta così?** | Is that enough?/Is that all? |
| **Va bene così?** | Is that OK? |
| **Nient'altro?/Dopo?** | Anything else? |
| **Mi dispiace, non ne abbiamo** | I'm sorry, we haven't any |
| **stamattina/per oggi** | this morning/today |
| **Abbiamo . . .** | We have . . . |

# 3 SHOPPING, FOOD

*Asking for what you want (For a list of food items see p. 81)*

| | |
|---|---|
| Vorrei . . . | I'd like . . . |
| un chilo di mele rosse | a kilo of red apples |
| mezzo chilo di pere | half a kilo of pears |
| Ha dell'uva bianca? | Do you have any white grapes? |
| Ne vorrei un chilo e mezzo | One and a half kilos (of them) |
| due chili di pomodori maturi | two kilos of ripe tomatoes |
| Vorrei del maiale | I'd like some pork |
| Abbiamo vitello, manzo, agnello | We have veal, beef, lamb |
| Mi dà del vitello | Give me some veal |
| Lo vorrei tenero e magro | I'd like it tender and lean |
| Quattro etti di carne buona | 400 grams of good meat |
| Ha del salame nostrano? | Do you have some local salami? |
| della mortadella | some spiced pork sausage? |
| due etti di prosciutto crudo/cotto | 200 grams of cured ham/cooked ham |
| Che formaggio ha? | What cheese do you have? |
| della mozzarella/della ricotta | mild cheese for pizzas/curd cheese |
| del Bel Paese/del gorgonzola | Bel Paese/Gorgonzola (blue) cheese |
| dell'olio/dello zucchero | some oil/some sugar |
| del burro/degli spaghetti | some butter/some spaghetti |
| un litro di latte | a litre of milk |
| sei uova | half a dozen eggs |
| il pane | bread |
| del pane casereccio | farmhouse bread |
| una focaccia/un panino | round loaf/bread roll |
| Mi dà un sacchetto di plastica | A plastic carrier-bag please |

## the way it works

### Some and any

Look at the following examples:

| | |
|---|---|
| Vorrei **del** maiale | I'd like some pork |
| **dell'**olio . . . **dello** zucchero | some oil . . . some sugar |
| **della** mozzarella/**degli spaghetti** | some mozzarella/some spaghetti |

Use the word for 'of' (**di**) together with 'the' (**il, la,** etc.). Check the table on p. 16 for the combinations of **di** and definite articles.

Note that to say 'I want some of it' you use **Ne vorrei**. And if the shopkeeper hasn't any he will say **Non ne abbiamo.**

### Saying how much you want

When buying food you will need to be able to ask for specific weights and measures. One very useful weight in Italy is the **etto** (hectogram = 100 grams). Many items can be bought by the **etto** (plural **etti**):

| | |
|---|---|
| **quattro etti** di carne buona | 400 grams of good meat |
| **due etti** e mezzo di salame | 250 grams of salami |

# 3  SHOPPING, FOOD

Other ways of specifying how much you want include:

**un po' di**
  formaggio        a little cheese
**una dozzina di** uova   a dozen eggs
**cinque fette** di       5 slices of ham
  prosciutto
**una bottiglia di**      a bottle of wine
  vino
**una scatola di**        a box of chocolates
  cioccolatini
**un pacchetto di**      a packet of
  sigarette          cigarettes

## *Paying up (For numbers see p. 78)*

Understanding the amount to pay is not always easy when hundreds and thousands
of lire are frequently used:

quattrocentocinquanta    450 lire     quattromilacinquecento    4.500 lire
milletrecentocinquanta   1.350 lire   undicimilaseicento       11.600 lire

You will sometimes hear a shortened form: **Undicimilaseicento lire** can also be
called **undici e sei**. In other words, the words **mila** (thousands) and **cento** (hundred)
are taken out and the thousands, hundreds and units are linked by **e** (and). Thus 450
lire can be called **quattro e cinquanta**.

## *things to do*

3.1   Before going shopping, Anna is going over in her mind all the items
     she needs to buy. Can you complete her list for her (using **del, dell',
     dello, dei, delle, degli**):
     . . . pane casereccio, . . . mele e pere, . . . uva bianca, . . . pomodori,
     . . . maiale, . . . prosciutto, . . . spaghetti, . . . formaggio, . . . olio, . . .
     zucchero.

3.2   It's your turn to do the shopping! Can you ask for each item on the
     list starting **Mi dà** or **Vorrei**:

> 200 grams butter (burro)
> 1 litre milk (latte)
> 1 bottle white wine (vino bianco)
> ½ kilo coffee (caffè)
>
> 1 kilo spaghetti (spaghetti)
> 2 kilos red apples (mele)
> 1½ kilos ripe tomatoes (pomodori)

3.3   Can you work out in Italian the prices of the following items:
     Quattro cartoline? Sono . . .     Due francobolli? Sono .

 L200      L600

     Un giornale inglese? È . . .     Due scatole di cioccolatini? Sono . . .

 L1500      L3300

# 3  RESTAURANTS

## ORDERING A MEAL

**Closing days**   Many restaurants and bars close one day a week in turn on a rota system (**chiusura per turno**). In addition to the normal closing day, you may find a sign in the summer (particularly during August) which indicates holiday closing (**Chiuso per ferie**) which means the establishment could well be closed for several weeks.

**Restaurants**   For a full meal, choose between a **ristorante** (formal restaurant, graded by stars, forks, etc.) or a **trattoria** (medium-priced meals, often very good value). For less expensive or lighter meals look for a **rosticceria** (ready-cooked food such as spit-roasted chicken), a **tavola calda** (inexpensive hot dishes, often crowded), or, of course, a **pizzeria**, where you can either eat on the premises or buy a take-away portion (**pizza al taglio**) to eat at home. The bill (**il conto**) usually includes a cover charge (**pane e coperto**) and service (**il servizio**), but many people give an extra tip for really good food and service. The restaurant must give you a receipt (**una ricevuta fiscale**) which may be checked by tax officials.

**Menus**   You will usually find in addition to the à la carte dishes a **menù a prezzo fisso** (set menu) or a **menù turistico** (tourist menu). There may be a **piatto del giorno** (dish of the day) and the chef will often recommend his speciality – **la specialità della casa**.

## cosa prendono?/what'll you have?

Raffaella is joined by her student sister Giulia and together with Paul they go to have lunch at a restaurant – the Olivi in Via delle Terme.

Cameriere:   Buongiorno, signori, quanti sono?
Raffaella:   **Siamo** in tre.

# 3 RESTAURANTS

| | |
|---|---|
| Cameriere: | C'è un tavolo vicino alla finestra. (They sit down) Va bene? |
| Raffaella: | Sì, grazie. **Potremmo avere il menù**, per favore? |
| Cameriere: | Subito, signori. |
| | (A little later) Cosa prendono, signori? |
| Raffaella: | Allora, io vorrei **per primo** una minestra di funghi, e **di secondo** fegato alla veneziana. |
| Cameriere: | Va bene. E di contorno? |
| Raffaella: | **Mi porti** dei fagiolini, per favore. E per te, Giulia? |
| Giulia: | **A me porti** dei tortellini e una cotoletta alla milanese. **Per contorno** prendo un po' di spinaci. |
| Paul: | **Per me** delle fettuccine alle vongole e di secondo una bistecca alla fiorentina, per favore. E come contorno, vorrei degli zucchini e delle patate fritte. |
| Cameriere: | E la bistecca, come la vuole – al sangue, ben cotta? |
| Paul: | Al sangue. |
| Cameriere: | Benissimo, signore. E da bere? |
| Raffaella: | (to Paul) **Prendiamo** del vino bianco e anche del rosso, vero? |
| Paul: | Sì, va bene. |
| Raffaella: | **Una bottiglia** di Frascati, per favore, e anche mezzo litro di Orvieto. Oh . . . e **ci può portare anche** una bottiglia di acqua minerale? |

**Meals and mealtimes** Traditionally lunch (**il pranzo**) is the main meal of the day and is eaten between midday and about 3pm. In the cities, however, many people take a shorter time for lunch and have a lighter meal. The evening meal (**la cena**) is served from about 7 or 8pm.

## Desiderano altro? (Anything else?)

Raffaella, Giulia and Paul have reached the dessert stage.

| | |
|---|---|
| Cameriere: | È andato tutto bene? |
| Paul: | **Molto bene, grazie.** |
| Cameriere: | Desiderano altro? Abbiamo torta della casa, zabaglione . . |
| Rafaella: | Niente dolce per me. Un caffè ristretto, per favore. |
| Cameriere: | E per la signorina? |
| Giulia: | **Avete gelati?** |
| Cameriere: | Sì, abbiamo cassata e gelati assortiti. |
| Giulia: | Una cassata **va bene per me.** |
| Paul: | Io vorrei del formaggio e un caffè lungo. E **posso avere il conto?** |
| Cameriere: | Sì, signore, lo porto subito. |

| | |
|---|---|
| **Vorrei riservare un tavolo per sei** | I'd like to reserve a table for six |
| **Avete un tavolo per quattro?** | Do you have a table for four? |
| **un'altra sedia?** | another chair? |
| **Quanti sono?** | How many are you? |
| **un tavolo vicino alla finestra** | a table near the window |
| **. . .sulla terrazza/nell'angolo** | . . . on the terrace/in the corner |

# 3  RESTAURANTS

## Ordering a meal

| | |
|---|---|
| Potremmo avere il menù? | Can we have the menu? |
| Cosa consiglia? | What do you recommend? |
| Antipasti | Hors d'oeuvres |
| Primi piatti/Secondi piatti | First courses/Second courses |
| per primo/come secondo | as a first course/for second course |
| Vorrei una frittata | I'd like an omelette |
| . . . di spinaci/di formaggio | . . . spinach/cheese |
| Contorni/Desserts | Vegetables/Desserts |
| Verdure di stagione/Contorno a scelta | Vegetables in season/Choice of vegetables |
| per contorno/come dessert | as a vegetable/for dessert |
| È possibile avere . . .? | Is it possible to have . . .? |
| Anche per te? | For you too? |
| La prendo anch'io | I'll have it too |
| Come sono gli spaghetti? | How is the spaghetti prepared? |
| La bistecca, come la vuole? | How do you like your steak? |
| al sangue/ben cotta | rare/well done |
| Da bere? | What would you like to drink? |
| una bottiglia di/mezzo litro di | a bottle of/a half litre of |
| Ci può portare . . .? | Could you bring us . . .? |
| acqua minerale | mineral water |
| Niente dolce per me | Nothing sweet for me |
| Avete gelati? | Do you have ice-creams? |
| Abbiamo cassata | We have cassata (ice-cream with candied fruit) |
| gelati assortiti | assorted ice-creams |
| alla fragola/al limone/alla vaniglia | strawberry/lemon/vanilla flavour |
| Vorrei del formaggio | I'd like some cheese |
| torta di cioccolata | chocolate cake |
| Prendo un caffè ristretto | I'll have a strong black coffee |
| un caffè lungo | large weaker black coffee |
| Posso avere il conto? | Please could I have the bill? |
| Dov'è la toilette? | Where is the toilet? |

## *Posso avere un coltello? (May I have a knife?)*

# 3 RESTAURANTS

## the way it works

### Ways of asking for something to be brought

Note the following:
| | |
|---|---|
| Per me . . . | For me . . . |
| Mi porti . . . | Bring me . . . |

Also:
| | |
|---|---|
| Posso avere . . .? | Could I have . . .? |
| Ci può portare . . .? | Could you bring us . . .? |
| Potremmo avere . . .? | Could we have . . .? |

### Direct object pronouns (1)

| | |
|---|---|
| La bistecca? Come la vuole? | The steak? How do you want it (done)? |
| Il conto? Lo porto subito. | The bill? I'll bring it at once. |

The word for 'it' is **lo** for a masculine noun and **la** for a feminine noun. Use **l'** for a noun beginning with a vowel. In the plural use **li** and **le** for 'them'. Note also that **lo, la, li, le** can refer to people as well as objects.
Object pronouns usually come *before* the verb:

| | |
|---|---|
| Il cameriere? Lo vedo. | The waiter? I see him. |

The full list of unstressed direct object pronouns is as follows:

| | *singular* | | *plural* |
|---|---|---|---|
| mi | me | ci | us |
| ti | you (familiar) | vi | you |
| la | you (formal) | le | you (formal) |
| lo | him/it | li | them (masc.) |
| la | her/it | le | them (fem.) |

### Direct object pronouns (2)

These stressed object pronouns are used only after a word such as **a** or **per**.

| | |
|---|---|
| Per me va bene. | That's fine for me. |
| Anche per te? | And for you, too? |

| | *singular* | | *plural* |
|---|---|---|---|
| me | me | noi | us |
| te | you (familiar) | voi | you |
| lei | you (formal)/her | loro | them |
| lui | him | | |

Note that with the exception of **me** and **te**, they are identical to the subject pronouns.

### Regular verbs: group 2 (prendere)

The verb **prendere** (to have or take) is an example of the second group of regular Italian verbs (infinitive **-ere**). Here is its full pattern in the present tense:

| *singular* | | *plural* | |
|---|---|---|---|
| prend**o** | I take | prend**iamo** | we take |
| prend**i** | you take (familiar) | prend**ete** | you take |
| prend**e** | he/she/it takes, you take | prend**ono** | they take |

# 3   RESTAURANTS

## *Formal 'you' (plural)*

In this unit you may have noticed that the waiter uses the formal third person form when addressing his customers together. **Cosa prendono?** (What will you have?), **Desiderano altro?** (Would you like anything else?). This formal form is still quite normal usage from a waiter in a good restaurant, but it has virtually disappeared from ordinary speech.

## things to do

3.4   Sitting at your restaurant table you find you need to ask for quite a few things. Use **Avete . . .?** or **Mi porti . . .**
   1  Please could you have another chair.
   2  You'd like the salt and pepper.
   3  You want to know if they have roast chicken on the menu.
   4  You want to know if they have chips.

3.5   You arrive at a restaurant with two friends.

| | |
|---|---|
| Waiter: | Buona sera, quanti sono? |
| You: | [Say you are three. Ask if he has a table] |
| Waiter: | Sì. Questo tavolo va bene? |
| You: | [Yes, that's fine.] |
| Waiter: | Cosa prendono, signori? |
| You: | [For the lady: fish soup and a veal cutlet in marsala sauce] [For the gentleman: tagliatelle with clams and a grilled steak] [For yourself: baked cannelloni and chicken breasts] |
| Waiter: | Va bene, e per contorno? |
| You: | [Ask him to bring some courgettes and some mushrooms] |
| Waiter: | E da bere? |
| You: | [Say you'd like a bottle of Orvieto] |
| Waiter: | Subito, signori. |

### MENÙ

#### *Antipasti:*

| | |
|---|---|
| Insalata di frutti di mare | Seafood salad |
| Prosciutto con melone | Cured ham and melon |

#### *Primi piatti:*

| | |
|---|---|
| Minestra di funghi | Mushroom soup |
| Spaghetti alla carbonara | Spaghetti with egg & belly pork |
| Tortellini al pomodoro | Small, stuffed pasta shapes with tomato sauce |
| Tagliatelle alla vongole | Tagliatelle with clams |
| Cannelloni al forno | Baked cannelloni |

#### *Secondi piatti:*

| | |
|---|---|
| Cotolette alla romana | Veal cutlet in marsala sauce |
| Pollo alla cacciatora | Chicken in wine sauce with onions, tomatoes, peppers, etc |
| Bistecca alla fiorentina | Grilled steak with pepper |
| Fegato alla veneziana | Calves liver fried with onions |

#### *Contorni:*

| | |
|---|---|
| Zucchini/Fagiolini/Spinaci | Courgettes/French beans/Spinach |
| Insalata mista/verde | Mixed/green salad |

## CHANGING MONEY

**Banks** are open Monday to Friday except on public holidays. The hours are from about 8.30 or 9am till about 12.30 or 1pm. They are sometimes open for an hour in the afternoons between about 3 and 4pm. In city centres most banks will cash Eurocheques. Traveller's cheques may also be accepted by some hotels and many shops, but you will get a better rate of exchange at a bank.

**Money**   Banknotes (**i biglietti**) come in denominations of 1.000, 2.000, 5.000, 10.000, 50.000 and 100.000 lire. There are coins of 10, 20, 50, 100, 200 and 500 lire. Credit cards are becoming more widely accepted in hotels, restaurants and shops and in some petrol-stations. Most people, however, still use cash.

### vado in banca/I'm going to the bank

Paul wants to go to Venice the next day for a music festival and Giulia is going with him. She has come to see Paul who has plans for the morning.

| | |
|---|---|
| Giulia: | Ciao, Paul. **Cosa fai** stamattina? |
| Paul: | Prima **vado in banca** e poi alla Stazione Centrale. **Vado a fare il biglietto** per Venezia per domani mattina. |
| Giulia: | Posso accompagnarti? |
| Paul: | Certo! |
| (They arrive at the bank) | |
| Impiegato: | Desidera, signore? |

# 4 USING PUBLIC TRANSPORT

Paul:      Buongiorno. **Vorrei incassare questi tre travellers cheques. Quant'è il cambio della sterlina?**

Impiegato:      La sterlina è a duemila lire. Mi dà il suo passaporto, per favore. (Paul hands it over) . . . E firmi qui . . . Grazie. Come vuole i soldi?

Paul:      Vorrei **un biglietto da centomila** e due da diecimila. (Clerk gives him the money) Grazie.

Impiegato:      Prego.

## *USEFUL WORDS AND PHRASES*

| | |
|---|---|
| **Cosa fai stamattina?** | What are you doing this morning? |
| **Primo . . . poi** | First . . . then |
| **vado in banca/alla stazione** | I'm going to the bank/to the station |
| **vado a fare il biglietto** | I'm going to buy a ticket |
| **domani mattina** | tomorrow morning |
| **Posso accompagnarti?** | Can I come with you? |
| **Certo!** | Certainly, with pleasure |

### *At the bank*

| | |
|---|---|
| **Vorrei incassare . . .** | I'd like to cash . . . |
| **. . . questo travellers cheque** | . . . this traveller's cheque |
| **. . . un eurocheque** | . . . a Eurocheque |
| **Mi può cambiare . . .?** | Can you change . . .? |
| **. . . cento sterline** | . . . £100 |
| **. . . un assegno (di conto corrente)** | . . . a personal cheque |
| **Ho una carta di credito** | I have a credit card |
| **Quant'è il cambio della sterlina?** | What is the exchange rate of the pound? |
| **La sterlina è a . . .** | The pound is at . . . |
| **Firmi qui** | Sign here |
| **Come vuole i soldi?** | How do you want your money? |
| **Un biglietto da ventimila** | One 20.000 lire note |
| **Vorrei aprire un conto** | I want to open an account |
|      **versare questo** |      credit this |
|      **prelevare . . . lire** |      withdraw . . . lire |
| **Ha degli spiccioli?** | Do you have any small change? |

# 4 USING PUBLIC TRANSPORT

## BUYING A TRAIN TICKET

**Trains**  Train travel is generally cheap and comfortable and there are many different types of train and variations in fares, so it is worth being specific when asking for information. The main types are as follows:

**Super-rapido or TEE:** Luxury first-class-only trains running between main Italian cities. You pay a supplement and you must book a seat.
**Rapido:** Fast inter-city trains, some of which are first-class only. You pay a supplement and for some trains it is obligatory to book a seat.
**Expresso:** Long-distance trains stopping at main stations. Both classes.
**Diretto:** Trains stopping at most stations.
**Locale:** Trains stopping at all stations.

Children under four travel free and from four to twelve pay half fare. There are several forms of reduced fare available to tourists, both individually and in groups.

**Metro**  There are underground networks (**la metropolitana**) in Rome and Milan. Fares are charged on a flat-fare system.

## a che ora parte?/what time does it leave?

Next, Paul and Giulia go to the station. Paul asks a passer-by how to get there.

Paul:         Scusi, **come si fa per andare alla stazione** centrale?
Passante:   Va a piedi, vero? Così fa più presto. Allora, prenda la Via dei Serragli, passi per la Piazza Goldoni e vada sempre diritto.
Paul:         Grazie.

# 4 USING PUBLIC TRANSPORT

Arriving at the station, Paul and Giulia go to the enquiry desk (**l'ufficio informazioni**) to find out the times of the trains to Venice.

| | |
|---|---|
| Paul: | Buongiorno. **Vorrei sapere l'orario dei treni** per Venezia. **C'è un treno diretto**, o devo cambiare? |
| Impiegata: | È diretto. Quando vuole partire? |
| Paul: | **Domani mattina.** |
| Impiegata: | Domani mattina? C'è un rapido che parte alle dieci e venticinque. Arriva a Venezia alle tredici e trentasette. |
| Paul: | **Quanto costa il biglietto?** |
| Impiegata: | Andata o andata e ritorno? |
| Paul: | Solo **andata, seconda classe.** |
| Impiegata: | Allora sono quarantamila lire. |
| Paul: | **C'è vettura ristorante?** |
| Impiegata: | Sì, signore. |

### How does one get there?

| | |
|---|---|
| **Come si fa per andare a . . .?** | How does one get to . . .? |
| **Va a piedi** | You are walking |
| **Così (lei) fa più presto** | You'll get there more quickly |

Next they go to the ticket-office.

| | |
|---|---|
| Paul: | **Mi dà due biglietti di andata sul rapido** di domani mattina per Venezia, per favore? |
| Impiegato: | In prima o seconda classe? |
| Paul: | Seconda. |
| Impiegato: | Va bene. (He gives Paul the ticket) Quarantamila lire. |
| Paul: | (He pays) **Il treno parte alle dieci** e venticinque, vero? |
| Impiegato: | Esatto. |
| Paul: | **Su che binario arriva?** |
| Impiegato: | Sul primo binario. |

### Train enquiries

| | |
|---|---|
| **Vorrei sapere l'orario . . .** | I'd like to find out the timetable |
| **. . . dei treni per Venezia** | . . . of trains to Venice |
| **C'è un treno diretto?** | Is there a through train? |
| **Devo cambiare?** | Do I have to change? |
| **C'è una coincidenza per . . .?** | Is there a connection to . . .? |
| **Si ferma a Palermo** | It stops at Palermo |
| **Quando vuole viaggiare?** | When do you want to travel? |
| **Domani mattina** | Tomorrow morning |
| **Quando parte il prossimo treno per . . .?** | When is the next train to . . .? |
| **C'è un rapido** | There's a *rapido* |
| **Il treno parte a . . .** | The train leaves at . . . |
| **A che ora arriva a Venezia?** | What time does it arrive in Venice? |

# 4 USING PUBLIC TRANSPORT

| | |
|---|---|
| Torno in giornata | I'm coming back the same day |
| dopodomani | the day after tomorrow |
| C'è vettura ristorante? | Is there a restaurant-car? |
| Su che binario arriva? | What platform does it come in on? |

### Buying a train ticket

| | |
|---|---|
| Mi dà due biglietti per . . . | I'd like two tickets to . . . |
| un biglietto chilometrico | reduced ticket valid for 3000 km. |
| metà tariffa | half-fare |
| andata/andata e ritorno | single/return ticket |
| prima classe/seconda classe | first/second class |
| Vorrei prenotare un posto | I'd like to book a seat |

### Attenzione! Attenzione! (Listen for the following phrases)

| | |
|---|---|
| È in arrivo sul binario quattro . . . | Arriving at platform 4 . . . |
| Il treno da.../per... | The train from.../for... |
| Ha circa cinque minuti di ritardo | It's about 5 minutes late |
| L'arrivo è previsto alle . . . | It's expected to arrive at . . . |

## the way it works

### Cosa fai? (What are you doing?)

**Fare** (to do, make) is also used in many colloquial phrases:

| | |
|---|---|
| Vado a **fare** il biglietto. | I'm going to buy a ticket. |
| Come **si fa** per . . .? | How does one get to . . .? (lit. one do?) |

The present tense of this verb is irregular:

| | | | |
|---|---|---|---|
| **faccio** | I do, make | **facciamo** | we do, make |
| **fai** | you do (familiar) | **fate** | you do |
| **fa** | he/she does, you do (formal) | **fanno** | they do |

### Vado . . .

We have already met several phrases which use parts of the verb **andare** (to go)

| | |
|---|---|
| **Vado** in banca. | I'm going to the bank. |
| **Va** bene. | OK. (lit. it goes well) |
| **Andiamo** a casa. | We are going home. |

Like **fare**, the present tense of this verb is irregular:

| | | | |
|---|---|---|---|
| **vado** | I go | **andiamo** | we go |
| **vai** | you go (familiar) | **andate** | you go |
| **va** | he/she goes, you go (formal) | **vanno** | they go |

### Regular verbs: group 3 (preferire/partire)

There are two patterns of regular -**ire** verbs, as shown in the following examples:

| | | | |
|---|---|---|---|
| prefer**isco** | I prefer | prefer**iamo** | we prefer |
| prefer**isci** | you prefer (fam.) | prefer**ite** | you prefer |
| prefer**isce** | he/she prefers, you prefer | prefer**iscono** | they prefer |

# 4 USING PUBLIC TRANSPORT

**Partire** (to leave) follows a different pattern:
A che ora **parte** il prossimo treno?     What time does the next train leave?

| | | | |
|---|---|---|---|
| part**o** | I leave | part**iamo** | we leave |
| part**i** | you leave (familiar) | part**ite** | you leave |
| part**e** | he/she/it leaves, you leave | part**ono** | they leave, you leave |

Each time you come across a new **-ire** verb you need to learn which pattern it follows.

## things to do

**4.1**  You are in a bank and you want to change some money.

You:    [Say good morning. You'd like to change £50 pounds]
Clerk:  Ha il passaporto, per favore?
You:    [Yes, here it is. Ask what the exchange rate is]
Clerk:  È a duemilatrecento lire. Firmi qui, per favore e passi alla
        cassa. Vuole un biglietto da centomila?
You:    [No. Ask to be given two L50.000 notes]
Clerk:  Ecco a lei. Grazie e buongiorno.

**4.2**  You overhear a booking-clerk advising a passenger about trains.
Can you guess what the passenger is asking?

Passenger:  ...................................................................................................?
Clerk:      Il prossimo treno per Milano parte alle nove a trenta.
Passenger:  ...................................................................................................?
Clerk:      Arriva alle tredici e quindici.
Passenger:  ...................................................................................................?
Clerk:      Deve cambiare a Padova.
Passenger:  ...................................................................................................?
Clerk:      Andata o andata e ritorno?
Passenger:  ...................................................................................................?

**4.3**  **A che ora parte il treno per . . .?** You are at Milan station with a group
of tourists, each of whom wants to go to a different Italian city. Can
you say when each train leaves and when it arrives?

| | **PARTENZE** | **ARRIVI** |
|---|---|---|
| *Bologna* | 9:15 | 11:45 |
| *Torino* | 10:20 | 12:50 |
| *Firenze* | 11:30 | 15:30 |
| *Ancona* | 12:02 | 18:00 |
| *Roma* | 13:40 | 21:30 |

# 4 USING PUBLIC TRANSPORT

## TAKING THE BUS

**L'autobus**   Buses are the only form of public transport in most Italian cities. Fares are normally charged on a flat-fare basis. You often have to buy tickets in advance from a news kiosk (**un'edicola**) or tobacconist's. Sometimes you pay at the bus stop either by putting the exact change into a ticket dispenser or by putting a special ticket-card (**una tesserina**) into a hole-punching machine.

**Il pullman** (coach), **la corriera** (country bus): There is an extensive coach and bus network covering every part of Italy.

## per andare a . . .?/how do I get to . . .?

Marisa decides to visit a famous church on a hill outside Florence. She asks a passer-by for advice:

Marisa:     Per piacere, **per andare** a San Miniato al Monte, **devo prendere l'autobus?**

Passante:   Sì, signorina. Deve prendere il 13 e scendere al Piazzale Michelangelo.

Marisa:     **Mi puo dire dov'è la fermata** del 13, per favore?

Passante:   Allora . . . Vada fino al semaforo. Attraversi la strada e giri a destra. La fermata è lì sulla destra.

Marisa:     Ho capito. **Ogni quanto passano gli autobus?**

Passante:  Ogni dieci minuti, credo.
Marisa:    E mi può dire **quanto tempo ci vuole?**
Passante:  Circa quindici minuti . . . Non lo so esattamente.
Marisa:    Grazie mille.
Passante:  Prego.

## *Going by bus*

| | |
|---|---|
| Dov'è la stazione degli autobus? | Where is the bus-station? |
| Devo prendere l'autobus? | Should I take the bus? |
| C'è un autobus? | Is there a bus? |
| Che numero devo prendere? | What number should I take? |
| Deve prendere il 13 e scendere a . . . | You should take the 13 and get off at . . |
| Dov'è la fermata del 13? | Where is the No. 13 bus-stop? |
| Vada fino al semaforo | Go to the traffic-lights |
| Attraversi la strada | Cross the street |
| Giri a destra | Turn right |
| La fermata si trova sulla destra | The stop is on the right |
| Sa ogni quanto passano? | Do you know how often they run? |
| Ogni venti minuti, credo | Every 20 minutes, I think |
| Mi può dire . . .? | Can you tell me? |
| . . . quanto tempo ci vuole? | . . . how long it (the journey) takes? |
| Circa quindici minuti | About 15 minutes |
| Non lo so esattamente | I don't know exactly |
| Mi può dire quando devo scendere? | Can you tell me when to get off? |
| Questa è la fermata per . . .? | Is this the stop for . . .? |
| Questo pullman si ferma a . . .? | Does this coach stop at . . .? |
| Quest' autobus va a a . . .? | Does this bus go to . . .? |

*(For departure times, etc. see section on Train Enquiries, p. 36)*

## MAKING A PHONE CALL

**Telephones**    The telephone service is almost completely automatic. Calls can be made from phone boxes (**la cabina telefonica**) or from a hotel. You can also make local calls from a café, where you sometimes need a token (**un gettone**). If you want to make an international call to Britain, dial 0044, then the area code *minus* the 0, then the number. The phonecard (**la carta telefonica**) is in widespread use.

# 4 PUBLIC TRANSPORT; TELEPHONE

## che ne pensi?/what do you think?

Back in the Lazzarinis' flat that evening, Giancarlo telephones a friend on the island of Elba to ask if he and Marisa can go and visit him this weekend.

| | |
|---|---|
| Marco: | **Pronto?** |
| Giancarlo: | **Qui parla** Giancarlo. Come stai, Marco? |
| Marco: | Bene, grazie, e tu? |
| Giancarlo: | **Benissimo**. Senti, Marco, Marisa e io pensiamo di visitarvi questo finesettimana. **Che ne pensi?** |
| Marco: | **Ottima idea**! Quando venite? |
| Giancarlo: | Domani sera – non so esattamente quando. Di passaggio vogliamo fermarci a Siena per pranzare e vedere le cose più interessanti. Prendiamo il traghetto alle cinque circa. Non mi ricordo quanto tempo ci mette . . . |
| Marco: | Circa un'ora. Va bene. **Allora a domani.** |
| Giancarlo: | Arrivederci. |

### Making plans

| | |
|---|---|
| pensiamo di . . . | we are thinking of . . . |
| visitarvi | visiting you |
| questo finesettimana | this weekend |
| Ottima idea! | Brilliant idea! |
| Quando venite? | When are you coming? |
| Domani sera | Tomorrow evening |
| Di passaggio | En route |
| vogliamo fermarci per pranzare | we want to stop for lunch |
| Prendiamo il traghetto | We'll take the ferry |
| Non mi ricordo… | I don't remember… |
| …quanto tempo ci mette/impiega | …how long it takes |

### Telephone talk

| | |
|---|---|
| Dov'è la cabina telefonica più vicina? | Where's the nearest phone-box? |
| Vorrei un gettone | I want a *token* |
| Qual è il prefisso per…? | What's the area code for . . .? |
| Mi può dare il numero di . . .? | Can you tell me the number for . . .? |
| Desidero il 40 25 58 di Roma | I want Rome 40 25 58 |
| un elenco telefonico | a telephone directory |
| Pronto. Sono . . . | Hello (*answering*). I am . . . |
| Qui parla . . . | This is . . . speaking |
| Chi parla? | Who's speaking? |
| Vorrei parlare a . . . | I want to speak to . . . |
| Un momento. Resti in linea. | One moment. Hold the line. |
| Può passare un messaggio? | Can you pass on a message? |
| Ha chiamato il numero sbagliato | You've got the wrong number |
| Il telefono non funziona | The phone isn't working |

41

# 4 USING PUBLIC TRANSPORT

## the way it works

### How are you travelling?

Note that you say *a piedi* (on foot). However, most forms of transport are preceded by **in** or **con**: **in** autobus, **con** l'autobus; **in** treno, **con** il treno.

| Vado | **in** autobus | I'm going by bus | Vado | **in** macchina | I'm going by car |
|---|---|---|---|---|---|
| | **in** aereo | by plane | | **in** tassì | by taxi |
| | **in** bicicletta | by bicycle | | **in** treno | by train |
| | **in** corriera | by coach | | **in** traghetto | by ferry |

You can also use **prendere** (to take): prendo l'aereo.

### Where are you going?

| Dove va per le vacanze? | Vado **in** Italia. | (with names of countries) |
|---|---|---|
| | Vado **a** Firenze. | (with names of towns, etc.) |

### Asking someone to do something for you

Note the expression **Mi può dire . . .?** (Can you tell me . . .?.) **Mi può** can be used with a variety of expressions:
**Mi può** cambiare questo travellers cheque?
**Mi può** dare un biglietto?
**Può** is part of the verb **potere** (to be able), whose present tense is as follows:

| **posso** | I can | **possiamo** | we can |
|---|---|---|---|
| **puoi** | you can (familiar) | **potete** | you can |
| **può** | he/she/it can, you can | **possono** | they can |

### Giving instructions

Not only will you want to be able to ask the way and understand directions, but you might also need to be able to give simple instructions yourself.

We have already met (Martedì mattina) words like **prenda** (take), **vada** (go), **giri** (turn), **passi per** (go along), which are forms of the verb known as the imperative (or command) form. Here we meet one more: **attraversi** (cross). The imperative is formed with the stem of the first person 'I' form and the following endings:
Regular **-are** verbs: **-i**
Regular **-ere** and **-ire** verbs: **-a**.
Note one other way in which you may be told politely what to do.
**Deve** prendere il autobus.     You must take the bus.
**Deve** is part of the verb **dovere** (to have to, must):

| **devo** | I must | **dobbiamo** | we must |
|---|---|---|---|
| **devi** | you must (familiar) | **dovete** | you must |
| **deve** | he/she must, you must | **devono** | they must |

### Reflexive verbs

**Non mi ricordo** (I don't remember) is an example of a verb which is being used reflexively, i.e. the subject acts upon, or does something to, himself or herself.

# 4  USING PUBLIC TRANSPORT

**Ricordare** means 'to remind' and thus the reflexive form **ricordarsi** means 'to remind oneself' or 'to remember'. The reflexive is formed by the addition of a special set of reflexive pronouns which, except in the infinitive, come before the verb, as follows:

| | | | |
|---|---|---|---|
| **mi** ricordo | I remember | **ci** ricordiamo | we remember |
| **ti** ricordi | you remember (fam) | **vi** ricordate | you remember (fam) |
| **si** ricorda | he/she remembers, you remember (formal) | **si** ricordano | they remember, |

Reflexive pronouns in some cases may be translated into English as 'oneself', etc.:
**Lavarsi** = to wash (oneself); **mi lavo** = I wash (myself).
**sposarsi** = to marry (someone); **incontrarsi** = to meet (one another)

## things to do

**4.4  Dove va in vacanza?** Where are you going for your holiday this year? Everyone is going somewhere different, and by a different means:

Carla:  Inghilterra          Antonio:  Napoli

Leo:  Francia          Giulia:  Orvieto

**4.5  At the coach station, you enquire about coaches to Milano.**

Bigliettaio: Buongiorno. Desidera?
You:  [Ask when the next coach to Milan leaves]
Bigliettaio: Parte alle undici e trenta.
You:  [Ask how long it takes]
Bigliettaio: Circa quattro ore.
You:  [Ask how much the ticket costs]
Bigliettaio: Andata o andata e ritorno?
You:  [Single]
Bigliettaio: Sono duemila quattrocento.
You:  [OK. Say you want a single ticket.]

**4.6  Come si fa per andare alla Posta?** Can you tell people how to get to various places?

| | |
|---|---|
| **1** La Posta? | [Take the first street on the right and it's on the left] |
| **2** La Banca Commerciale? | [Go to the traffic-lights and cross the road. It's just there, on the right] |
| **3** Fiesole | [You must take the bus. It takes about one hour. The stop is in the Piazza della Repubblica] |

# 5 MOTORING

## TRAVELLING BY CAR

**Documents**   A British driving-licence is valid in Italy but before you go you should obtain a translation of it from CIT (50 Conduit Street, London W1), or from the Italian State Tourist Office (1 Princes Street, London W1). If you take your own car, you should also have with you an International Green Card from your insurance company and the Vehicle Registration Book.

**Breakdowns**   If you do break down, dial 116 at the nearest telephone, tell the operator your whereabouts and the registration number and make of your car, and the ACI will come to your assistance. All vehicles must carry a yellow warning triangle which should be placed at least 50 metres behind the car.

**Highway code**   Italy adheres to the International Highway Code. It is compulsory to have a side mirror fitted on the left-hand side of the car. The wearing of seat-belts is strongly recommended. Note the following speed limits (for cars):

|  | to 600cc | to 900cc | to 1300cc | over 1300 cc |
|---|---|---|---|---|
| *Towns and villages:* | 50 km/h | 50 km/h | 50 km/h | 50 km/h |
| *Country roads:* | 80 | 90 | 100 | 110 |
| *Motorways:* | 90 | 110 | 130 | 140 |

# 5 MOTORING

*Some Italian road signs*

| | |
|---|---|
| Senso vietato ⎤ | No entry |
| Vietato l'accesso ⎦ | |
| Sosta vietata ⎤ | No parking |
| Divieto di sosta ⎦ | |
| Rallentare | Slow down |
| Svolta | Bend |
| Lavori stradali | Roadworks |
| Senso unico | One-way street |
| Zona di silenzio | No hooting |
| Precedenza a destra | Priority to vehicles coming from the right |
| Passaggio a livello | Level crossing |
| Divieto di sorpasso | No overtaking |
| Sosta autorizzata | Parking permitted (within certain times) |
| Deviazione | Diversion |
| Incrocio | Crossroads |
| Uscita/Entrata | Exit/Entrance |
| Soccorso ACI | ACI emergency service |
| Parcheggio limitato | Limited parking |

**Motorways** Italian motorways (**autostrade**) are well-engineered and cover most of the country, often running through spectacular scenery. The **Autostrada del Sole** (A1), which runs from Milan to Reggio di Calabria, is 1400 km long. You collect a ticket (**scontrino**) from the toll station (**casello**) and at your exit you pay a toll (**pedaggio**) based on the c.c. of your car and the distance covered.

**Parking** In town centres parking is limited and you will find that in blue zones you have to display a parking-disc (**disco di sosta**) which you set to show the time you arrived. These are available from petrol-stations.

*Breakdowns and repairs (For a list of parts of the car see p.82)*

| | |
|---|---|
| Ho un guasto alla macchina | My car has broken down |
| La mia macchina non parte | My car won't start |
| . . . non funziona molto bene | . . . isn't working |
| Il motore surriscalda | The engine is overheating |
| Dov'è il garage più vicino? | Where's the nearest garage |
| Può mandare un meccanico? | Can you send a mechanic? |
| Sono rimasto senza benzina | I've run out of petrol |
| Può riparare questa gomma? | Can you mend this tyre? |
| RIPARAZIONE GOMME | TYRE REPAIRS |
| Potrebbe cambiare le candele? | Could you change the plugs? |
| Il mio numero di immatricolazione è . . . | My registration number is . . . |

# 5 MOTORING

## il pieno, per favore/fill it up, please

Giancarlo and Marisa have set out for Siena in Giancarlo's Alfetta. Marisa wants a drink but Giancarlo is more concerned with finding a petrol-station (**una stazione di servizio**).

Marisa: Che caldo! Che ne dici di fermarci a bere qualcosa?
Giancarlo: Beh … Abbiamo bisogno di benzina. Cerco una stazione di servizio. (Suddenly he sees one) Ah! ce n'è una, là sulla destra.
(He drives in and stops)
Benzinaio: Quanti litri, signore?
Giancarlo: **Mi faccia il pieno**, per favore.
Benzinaio: Normale o super?
Giancarlo: **Super.** (The tank is filled) E **mi può controllare l'olio**, per piacere?
Benzinaio: Senz'altro. (He checks the oil) È un po' basso. Ne aggiungo un litro.
Giancarlo: Va bene. Allora quant'è?
Benzinaio: Quarantamilanovecento.
Giancarlo: Ecco a lei cinquantamila.
Benzinaio: Benissimo. Grazie e arrivederci.

# 5 MOTORING; EMERGENCY

| | |
|---|---|
| Abbiamo bisogno di benzina | We need petrol |
| una stazione di servizio | a service station |
| Quanti litri? | How many litres? |
| Quaranta litri | 40 litres |
| (Mi faccia) il pieno | Fill it up |
| normale o super | 2-star or 4-star |
| la benzina senza piombo | lead-free petrol |
| il gasolio | diesel |
| Mi può controllare l'olio? | Could you check the oil for me? |
| . . . la pressione delle gomme | . . . the tyre pressures |
| Senz'altro | Of course |
| È un po' basso | It's a bit low |
| Ne aggiungo un litro | I'll put in a litre |
| (Tutto) a posto | (All) in order, OK |

*USEFUL WORDS AND PHRASES*

| | |
|---|---|
| Che caldo! | How hot it is! |
| Che ne dici di . . .? | How about . . .? |
| bere qualcosa | to have something to drink |
| Cerco . . . | I'm looking for . . . |
| Ce n'è una | Here's one |

# COPING WITH LOSS OR THEFT

## ho perso il portafoglio/I have lost my purse

They set off again and haven't gone far before Marisa makes an unwelcome discovery . . .

Marisa: Oh no! Mi dispiace, Giancarlo, **ho perso il portafoglio**. Credo di averlo lasciato nella stazione di servizio

(Giancarlo stops the car)

Giancarlo: Ma come hai fatto a perderlo?

Marisa: Non sono sicura . . . Non mi ricordo.

Giancarlo: **Hai comprato una bibita?**

Marisa: Ah! Sì. Adesso mi ricordo. Ho comprato una bibita, e **ho messo** il portafoglio sulla cassa. Poi ho dimenticato di rimetterlo nella borsa.

Giancarlo: Non preoccuparti, non importa, ci torniamo subito. Anch'io ho fatto lo stesso **una settimana fa! Ho perso tutte le carte di credito** e non le ho più trovate.

# 5 MOTORING; EMERGENCY

## I have lost . . .!

| | |
|---|---|
| Ho perso il portafoglio | I've lost my purse/wallet |
| l'ho lasciato | I have left it |
| Come hai fatto a perderlo? | How did you lose it? |
| Non sono sicura | I'm not sure |
| Hai comprato una bibita? | Did you buy a drink? |
| Ho comprato | I bought |
| Ho messo il portafoglio sulla cassa | I put the purse on the cash desk |
| ho dimenticato di rimetterlo | I forgot to put it back |
| ci torniamo subito | we'll go back at once |
| ho fatto lo stesso | I did the same thing |
| una settimana fa | a week ago |
| ho perso tutte le carte di credito | I lost all my credit-cards |
| non le ho più trovate | I haven't found them |
| Mi è stato rubato il portafoglio | My wallet has been stolen |
| . . . la macchina fotografica | . . . my camera |
| . . . i miei oggetti di valore | . . . my valuables |
| Ho bisogno di fare la denuncia | I need to report to the police |
| Chiami la polizia! | Call the police! |

### USEFUL WORDS AND PHRASES

| | |
|---|---|
| Accidenti! | Bother! Damn! |
| Oddio! | Heavens! |
| Mi dispiace | I'm sorry |
| Non preoccuparti | Don't worry |
| Non importa | It doesn't matter |
| Meno male! | Thank goodness! |

## the way it works

### Saying what you did

When talking about a past action you use the perfect tense:

**Hai comprato** una bibita?          Did you buy a drink?

The perfect tense is formed by using part of the present tense of **avere** or **essere** followed by a past participle of the verb. Some verbs are preceded by **avere** and others by **essere**. Regular past participles are formed as follows:

**-are** verbs   drop **-are** and add **-ato**:   comprare, **comprato** (bought)
**-ire** verbs   drop **-ire** and add **-ito**:   partire, **partito** (left)
**-ere** verbs have no regular pattern – learn each one separately:

| | | | |
|---|---|---|---|
| bere (to drink) | **bevuto** | perdere (to lose): | **perso** |
| dovere (must, ought): | **dovuto** | prendere (to take): | **preso** |
| mettere (to put) | **messo** | volere (to want): | **voluto** |

# 5 MOTORING; EMERGENCY

## The perfect tense (using avere)

The majority of Italian verbs form their perfect tense with **avere**. Here is an example of the pattern of the perfect tense:

| | | | |
|---|---|---|---|
| **ho comprato** | I (have) bought | **abbiamo comprato** | we (have) bought |
| **hai comprato** | you (have) bought | **avete comprato** | you (have) bought |
| **ha comprato** | he/she (has) bought | **hanno comprato** | they (have) bought |
| | you (have) bought | | |

The ending of the past participle of these verbs is **-o** and does not change except when there is a feminine or plural object pronoun before it. These are **la, l'** (before a vowel or **h**), **li, le**:

Dov'è la borsa? **L**'ho mess**a** sulla tavola. (fem. singular)*

Ho perso tutte le carte di credito e non **le** ho più trovat**e**. (fem. plural)

*L' may be masculine or feminine, but the participle only changes its ending if the noun to which it refers is feminine.

## How to say you need something

**Abbiamo bisogno di benzina.**     We need petrol.

To express a need, use a part of the verb **avere** + **bisogno** (which doesn't change).

**Ho bisogno di una gomma.**     I need a tyre.

## things to do

**5.1** You are at a service-station. Say to the attendant in Italian:
1. that you want unleaded petrol
2. that you'd like 30 litres
3. could he please check the oil
4. . . . and check the tyre pressures.

**5.2** You see the following three street signs. What do they mean?
1. **Senso vietato**
   (a) No Parking  (b) No Entry  (c) One-Way Street
2. **Sosta vietata**
   (a) Roadworks  (b) No Parking  (c) Parking Permitted
3. **Divieto di sorpasso**
   (a) Diversion  (b) No Entry  (c) No Overtaking

**5.3** You can't find your camera and you go back to a café where you had a drink earlier.

| | |
|---|---|
| Direttore: | Buona sera, signore. Desidera? |
| You: | [You are sorry, but you think you left your camera here] |
| Direttore: | L'ha lasciata qui? Dove l'ha messa, signore? |
| You: | [Say you put the camera down on the table, bought a drink and then forgot to pick it up afterwards] |
| Direttore: | Un attimo . . . (he goes to look) Ce n'è una qui. È questa? |
| You: | [Say yes, that's yours and thank him very much] |

# 5  HEALTH AND EMERGENCY

## ILLNESS AND ACCIDENT

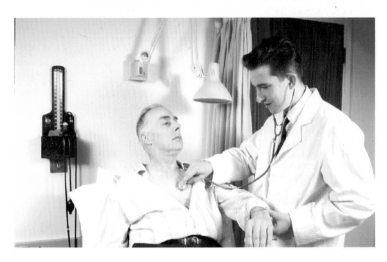

**Health**    As members of the EU, British visitors to Italy are entitled to the same health service as Italians. Before leaving for Italy you should obtain form E111 (available from post offices in the UK) to enable you to reclaim any medical bills paid in Italy. It is, however, advisable to take out private health insurance to give you full cover.

## mi sento male/I feel ill

Giancarlo's father, Enrico, hasn't been feeling well and goes to the doctor.

Medico:    Buongiorno, signore. Si sieda qui.
Enrico:    **Non mi sento molto bene,** dottore. **Mi fa male il torace.**
Medico:    Da quanto tempo le fa male?
Enrico:    Non sono sicuro. **Da circa due settimane** . . .
Medico:    Ha la febbre?
Enrico:    No, penso di no. Ma **ho mal di gola** e ho anche la tosse.
(The doctor examines his throat and chest)
Medico:    Apra la bocca . . . grazie. Adesso respiri profondamente . . . Ancora . . . . Va bene. Lei ha una bronchite. Le prescrivo un antibiotico. È allergico alla penicillina?
Enrico:    No.
Medico:    (writes a prescription) Allora, ecco una ricetta. Prenda una compressa tre volte al giorno prima di ogni pasto.
Enrico:    Grazie, dottore.

# 5 HEALTH AND EMERGENCY

*Diagnosis . . . (For parts of the body see p.81–2)*

| | |
|---|---|
| Si sieda qui | Sit down here |
| Non mi sento molto bene | I don't feel very well |
| Mi sento male | I feel ill |
| Dove fa male? | Where does it hurt? |
| Mi fa male il torace | My chest is hurting |
| Mi fa male il/la . . . | My . . . hurts |
| Da quanto tempo le fa male il . . .? | How long has your . . . been hurting? |
| Da quanto tempo si sente male? | How long have you been feeling ill? |
| Da circa due settimane | For about two weeks |
| Ha la febbre? | Do you have a temperature? |
| Penso di no | I don't think so |
| Ho mal di gola . . . e ho la tosse | I have a sore throat . . . and a cough. |
| Ho la diarrea | I have diarrhoea |
| Ho vomitato | I've been sick |
| Apra la bocca | Open your mouth |
| Respiri profondamente | Breathe deeply |
| Ancora | Again |
| Lei ha una bronchite | You have bronchitis |

*. . . and prescription*

| | |
|---|---|
| Le prescrivo . . . | I'll prescribe . . . |
| . . . un antibiotico | . . . an antibiotic |
| Lei è allergico alla penicillina? | Are you allergic to penicillin? |
| Sono allergico agli antibiotici | I'm allergic to antibiotics |
| Che medicina prende? | What medicine are you on? |
| Sono incinta (di 3 mesi) | I'm (3 months) pregnant |
| Prendo la pillola | I'm on the pill |
| Ho il diabete | I have diabetes |
| Deve andare all'ospedale | You must go to hospital |
| Voglio che faccia una radiografia | I'd like you to have an X-ray |
| Deve restare a letto | You must stay in bed |
| Ecco una ricetta | Here's a prescription |
| Prenda una compressa . . . | Take one pill . . . |
| tre volte al giorno | three times a day |
| prima di/dopo ogni pasto | before/after meals |

**Chemists** Chemist shops have a green or red cross outside and are easily recognised. At every shop, there is a list of those in the vicinity which are open at nights or on Sundays.

FARMACIA

*At the chemist's (For chemist items see p.80)*

| | |
|---|---|
| Può darmi qualcosa per . . .? | Can you give me something for . . . |
| . . . la febbre da fieno | . . . hay-fever |
| . . . le puncture d'insetti | . . . insect-bites |
| Sono stato punto | I've been stung |
| Ho un taglio/una contusione | I have a cut/a bruise |
| Ho una scottatura/una vescica | I have a burn/a blister |
| Ho mal di stomaco/mal d'orecchi | I have stomach-ache/earache |
| Ho mal di testa/mal di denti | I have a headache/toothache |

# 5 HEALTH AND EMERGENCY

| | |
|---|---|
| Ho un'indigestione/un colpo di sole | I have indigestion/sun-stroke |
| Mi può dare delle aspirine | Can you give me some aspirin? |
| Vorrei dei cerotti | I'd like some sticking-plasters |
| una benda (elastica) | (elastic) bandage |
| una crema solare | sun-tan cream |
| Quante volte al giorno . . .? | How many times a day . . .? |
| . . . devo prenderla | . . . should I take it |

*Medical notices*

| | |
|---|---|
| AMBULATORIO | DOCTOR'S SURGERY |
| PRONTO SOCCORSO | FIRST AID, EMERGENCY SERVICE |
| OSPEDALE | HOSPITAL |

## si è fatta male/she's hurt herself

After lunch Giancarlo and Marisa set off for the ferry but some miles into the countryside they come across an elderly lady who is lying at the side of the road beside her bicycle. Giancarlo stops the car . . .

Giancarlo: **Ha bisogno di aiuto**, signora?

Signora: Ai! **Mi sono fatta male** alla gamba. **Sono caduta** dalla bicicletta . . . e non posso muovere la gamba. Come mi fa male! Può chiamare mia figlia?

Giancarlo: Mi faccia vedere? (He takes a look) Signora, prima devo chiamare un'autoambulanza. Dov'è il telefono più vicino? Ah! C'è una casa lì in fondo – vado a telefonare. Tu, Marisa, rimani qui con la signora.

Marisa: (sits down beside her) Si calmi, signora, Giancarlo ritorna subito. Non si preoccupi.

(At the nearby house Giancarlo rings the doorbell)

52

# 5  HEALTH AND EMERGENCY

Giancarlo:  Posso usare il suo telefono, per favore?
Signore:  Entri pure! Che cosa è successo?
Giancarlo:  **C'è stato un incidente**. Una signora è caduta dalla bicicletta e
si è fatta male. Probabilmente **si è rotta** la gamba.... (dials)
...Pronto? Mi passi il pronto soccorso, per favore.

*Accidents and emergencies*

| | |
|---|---|
| Ha bisogno di aiuto? | Do you need help? |
| Mi sono fatta male alla gamba | I have hurt my leg |
| al braccio/alla testa | my arm/my head |
| Sono caduta dalla bicicletta | I fell off my bicycle |
| Non posso muovere la gamba | I can't move my leg |
| Come mi fa male! | It hurts so much! |
| Può chiamare mia figlia? | Can you ring my daughter? |
| Mi faccia vedere? | Would you let me see? |
| Devo chiamare un'autoambulanza | I must call an ambulance |
| Dov'è il telefono più vicino? | Where's the nearest telephone? |
| C'è una casa lì in fondo | There's a house over there |
| rimani qui | stay here (from *rimanere*) |
| Si calmi/Non si preoccupi | Calm yourself/Don't worry |
| Posso usare il suo telefono? | Can I use your telephone? |
| Entri pure! | Come in of course |
| Che cosa è successo? | What has happened? |
| C'è stato un incidente | There has been an accident |
| Probabilmente . . . | Probably . . . |
| . . . si è rotta la gamba | . . . she has broken her leg |
| . . . si è rotto il braccio | . . . he has broken his arm |
| Mi passì il pronto soccorso | Get me the emergency service |
| Lei deve andare in ospedale | You must go to hospital |
| Chiami un medico!/la Polizia! | Call a doctor/the Police! |
| la patente/l'assicurazione | driving-licence/insurance |
| nome e indirezzo | name and address |

## the way it works

### *I don't feel well!*

There are various ways in which you can describe your symptoms:

| | |
|---|---|
| Mi sento male | I feel ill |
| Non mi sento bene | I don't feel well |
| **Mi fa male** il torace | My chest is hurting (lit. it hurts to me the chest) |

Note that you do not use the possessive adjective (**mio,** etc.) when talking about parts of your body. **Mi** is an indirect object pronoun (to me).

| | |
|---|---|
| **Ho mal di** testa, etc. | I have a headache, etc. |
| **Ho** il raffreddore/la tosse | I have a cold/a cough |

Note that in Italian you say 'I have **the** cold', etc., not 'a' as in English.

# 5 HEALTH AND EMERGENCY

## Since when?

**Da quanto tempo** le fa male?          How long has it been hurting?
**Da** circa due settimane               For about two weeks
**Da** literally means 'since' in this context and is followed by the present tense.
**Da quanto tempo si sente** così?       How long have you been feeling like
                                         this? (lit. since how long do you feel
                                         thus?)

## The perfect tense (using essere)

Although most Italian verbs form their perfect tense with **avere**, there are some which use **essere**. These verbs are mostly those of movement, such as **andare** (to go). In such cases, the ending of the past participle has to agree with the subject of the verb and changes accordingly. Here is an example of a verb in the past tense formed with **essere**:

**sono andato/a**   I went            **siamo andati/e**   we went
**sei andato/a**    you went (fam)    **siete andati/e**   you went
**è andato/a**      he/she, you went  **sono andati/e**    they went

Here is a list of some of the most common verbs which use **essere**, together with their past participles:

| | | | | | |
|---|---|---|---|---|---|
| andare | (to go) | **andato** | venire | (to come) | **venuto** |
| arrivare | (to arrive) | **arrivato** | partire | (to leave) | **partito** |
| entrare | (to enter) | **entrato** | uscire | (to go out) | **uscito** |
| rimanere | (to remain) | **rimasto** | tornare | (to return) | **tornato** |
| scendere | (to go down) | **sceso** | cadere | (to fall) | **caduto** |

In addition, both **essere** and **stare** (to be) take **essere** in the perfect tense and their past participles are identical: **stato.**

Other verbs for which **essere** is needed in the perfect include all reflexives:
Mi sono                                  Ci siamo
  dimenticato/a    I forgot                ricordati/e      We remembered
Ti sei alzato/a    You got up           Vi siete lavati/e   You washed
Si è fatto male    He hurt himself      Si sono sentiti/e   They were taken
                                            male               ill

## Indirect object pronouns

Look at the following phrases:
**Mi** dà un chilo di mele               Give (to) me a kilo of apples
**Mi** passi il pronto soccorso          Pass the emergency service to me
**Le** prescrivo un antibiotico          I'll prescribe an antibiotic for you

In each case the pronoun (**mi, le**) is the indirect object and the prepositions 'for' or 'to' are either expressed or understood.

Here is the full list of indirect object pronouns:
| | | | |
|---|---|---|---|
| **mi** | (to/for) me | **ci** | (to/for) us |
| **ti** | (to/for) you (fam) | **vi** | (to/for) you |
| **le** | (to/for) you/her/ it | | |
| **gli** | (to/for) him/ it | **loro** | (to/for) them |

# 5 HEALTH AND EMERGENCY

## Position of object pronouns

Note that both direct and indirect pronouns normally come *before* the verb, except when they occur with an infinitive, in which case they may come *after* it and joined to it. Instances of this are common, occurring especially with combinations of verbs containing parts of the verbs **potere, volere** or **dovere**.

**Può** darmi la patente?      Can you give me your driving licence?
(Equally correct is: Mi può dare la patente?)
Non **voglio** dargli la patente      I don't want to give him my licence
**Deve** darmi la patente      You must give me your driving licence

When occurring with a perfect infinitive, the pronoun is added to the infinitive of **avere** or **essere**:

Penso di aver**lo** lasciato . . .      I think I left it . . .
Penso di aver**gli** dato la patente      I think I gave him my licence
Note that when a pronoun is added to an infinitive, the final **e** is left out.

## things to do

### 5.4 Dove fa male?

**5.5** The whole family has been in the wars! You consult the chemist.
1 Say you aren't feeling well. You have been sick and you have a stomach-ache.
2 Ask how often you should take the tablets.
3 Your daughter has fallen and hurt her knee (*il ginocchio*). Ask for an elastic bandage.
4 Your son has been stung by an insect. Ask if he can give you anything for insect bites.
5 You'd also like some sticking-plasters and some sun cream.

**5.6** Emergency! Can you report the following incidents to the police?
1 There has been an accident. A boy (*un ragazzo*) has fallen off his bike and has hurt his leg. Call a doctor quickly!
2 Your passport has been stolen. You left it in your room at the hotel yesterday but today it is no longer there.
3 A lady has been taken ill in the street. Send an ambulance!
4 You have lost your bag. You think you left it on the train.

# 6  SPORT AND LEISURE

## TALKING ABOUT SPORT / WEATHER

### che sport fai?/what sport do you do?

Marisa and Giancarlo are sitting having breakfast on the terrace of their friend's house in Elba discussing how to spend the day. Giancarlo is keen to try out his new sailboard.

Marco:     Allora, **cosa facciamo** oggi?
            Andiamo alla spiaggia?

Giancarlo: Certo. **Fa bel tempo** e voglio provare
            il mio nuovo surf. Ne potremmo
            noleggiare uno anche per te, Marisa.
            Che ne dici?

Marisa:     Ma **non so andare con il surf**. Non
            l'ho mai fatto.

Giancarlo: Puoi imparare. Posso mostrarti come
            si fa. Non è difficile – e **sai nuotare**,
            vero?

Marisa:     Abbastanza bene…Ma **oggi tira
            vento**…e l'acqua è ghiacciata!

Giancarlo: Non preoccuparti. **Proviamo un po'.**

(They continue talking about sport)

Marco:     D'estate che sport fai in Inghilterra, Marisa? Ti piace il tennis?

Marisa:     Sì, so giocare a tennis ma preferisco il nuoto. E d'inverno
            faccio lo sci. Vado a sciare sempre in Scozia con la mia
            famiglia, ma **fa spesso brutto tempo**.

Marco:     Davvero? Perchè non vieni qui in Italia? Ci sono delle piste
            favolose e in più **c'è anche il sole**.

Giancarlo: Ottima idea! L'anno prossimo andiamo tutti insieme.

# 6  SPORT AND LEISURE

*A matter of sport . . . (For a list of sports and equipment see p.82)*

| | |
|---|---|
| Andiamo alla spiaggia? | Shall we go to the beach? |
| Voglio provare il mio nuovo surf | I want to try out my new sailboard |
| Vuoi fare il bagno? | Do you want to have a swim? |
| Vorrei noleggiare . . . | I'd like to hire . . . |
| . . . un ombrellone | . . . a beach umbrella |
| . . . una barca a vela | . . . a sailing boat |
| Che ne dici? | What do you think? |
| Non so andare con il surf | I don't know how to sailboard |
| Posso mostrarti come si fa | I can show you how it's done |
| Preferisco il nuoto | I prefer swimming |
| Sai nuotare, vero? | You can swim, can't you? |
| So giocare a tennis/al calcio | I can play tennis/football |
| Si può andare a cavallo? | Can one go riding? |
| Vado a sciare | I go skiing |
| Mi piace far vela/pescare | I like sailing/fishing |

*. . . and weather*

| | |
|---|---|
| Le previsioni del tempo | weather forecast |
| Che tempo farà domani? | What will the weather be tomorrow? |
| Fa bel tempo | It's lovely weather |
|     brutto tempo |     bad weather |
| Fa caldo/fa freddo | It's hot/cold |
| C'è il sole | It's sunny |
| Il vento è forte/moderato | The wind is strong/moderate |
| Il mare è calmo/mosso/agitato | The sea is calm/rough/stormy |
| L'acqua è bella/ghiacciata | The water is lovely/freezing |
| la pioggia/la nebbia/la nuvola | rain/fog/cloud |
| Il cielo è coperto/sereno | The sky is overcast/clear |
| Piove/nevica/tira vento | It's raining/snowing/windy |
| Ci sono trenta gradi | It's 30 degrees |

# 6  SPORT AND LEISURE

*USEFUL WORDS AND PHRASES*

| | |
|---|---|
| sempre, mai, spesso | always, never, often |
| Proviamo un po' | Let's have a go |
| d'estate/d'inverno | in summer/in winter |
| la primavera/l'autunno | spring/autumn |
| Davvero? | Really? |
| Perchè non vieni . . .? | Why don't you come . . .? |
| tutti i giorni/tutti insieme | every day/all together |
| in più | moreover |

## SIGHTSEEING

**Museums and art galleries**    You normally pay an entrance fee for museums and galleries, unless you are under 18 or over 60. Museum opening times vary considerably so it is advisable to check at the local **ufficio turistico** or **azienda di soggiorno e turismo**. Most museums are closed on Mondays, and many churches are open only in the mornings.

## tante cose da vedere!/so much to see!

Paul has spent a busy morning sightseeing in Venice. He meets up with Giulia at a café.

Giulia:    Ciao! **Cosa hai visto** stamattina?
Paul:    Beh … mòlte cose! Ho preso il vaporetto per Piazza San Marco, **ho visitato** la Basilica, il Campanile e il Palazzo Ducale…
Giulia:    Cosa ne pensi? **Ti è piaciuto tutto?**
Paul:    **Moltissimo.** Ho visto dei quadri magnifici . . . Ma sono un po' stanco adesso! Vorrei visitare l'Accademia più tardi, dopo pranzo.
Giulia:    Che peccato! L'Accademia **è chiusa** il pomeriggio – **chiude all'una.** Ti conviene andare domani mattina.
Paul:    Sai **quando apre?**
Giulia:    Verso le otto e mezzo o le nove, credo.

# 6  SPORT AND LEISURE

Paul:    Va bene. Allora questo pomeriggio vorrei visitare la Chiesa dei Frari. Senti, cosa facciamo stasera?

Giulia:  Vuoi andare a un concerto? Danno un concerto di musica italiana del diciottesimo secolo. Che ne dici?

Paul:    **Mi piacerebbe molto**. Ma ci sono posti per questa sera?

Giulia:  Non lo so. Andiamo a vedere dopo pranzo.

## *Sightseeing*

| | |
|---|---|
| **Che cosa c'è da vedere?** | What is there to see? |
| **C'è tanto da vedere** | There's so much to see |
| **Cosa ha (i) visto?** | What have you seen? |
| **Ho preso il vaporetto** | I took the water-bus |
| **Cosa ne pensi?** | What do you think of it? |
| **Ti/Le è piaciuto tutto?** | Did you like it all? |
| **Moltissimo** | Very much indeed |
| **Ho visitato/Vorrei visitare** | I visited/I'd like to visit . . . |
| **Ho visto/Vorrei vedere** | I saw/I'd like to see |
| **la basilica, il campanile** | basilica, bell-tower |
| **la galleria, il museo** | gallery, museum |
| **la chiesa, il duomo** | church, cathedral |
| **dei quadri magnifici** | some magnificient pictures |
| | |
| **una mostra d'arte** | an art exhibition |
| **ENTRATA LIBERA** | ENTRANCE FREE |

## *Opening hours*

| | |
|---|---|
| **È chiuso(a)/è aperto(a)** | It is shut/open |
| **Chiude all'una** | It shuts at one |
| **Lunedì chiuso** | Shut on Mondays |
| **A che ora apre?** | What time does it open? |
| **Sai quando chiude?** | Do you know when it shuts? |
| **Ti conviene andare domani** | You'd better go tomorrow |

## *Plans for the evening*

| | |
|---|---|
| **Cosa facciamo stasera?** | What shall we do this evening? |
| **Vuoi andare . . .** | Do you want to go . . . |
| **. . . a un concerto?** | . . . to a concert? |
| **. . . al teatro/all'opera . . .** | . . . to the theatre/the opera? |
| **Danno un concerto** | There is a concert (lit. they give) |
| **musica del diciottesimo secolo** | eighteenth-century music |
| **Mi piacerebbe molto** | I'd like to very much |
| **Ci sono posti per questa sera?** | Are there seats for this evening? |
| **Andiamo a vedere** | We'll go and find out |
| **. . . dopo pranzo** | . . . after supper |

# 6 SPORT AND LEISURE

## the way it works
### Do you know how to . . .?

**Sapere** means 'to know' or 'to know about' something:

| | |
|---|---|
| Non lo **so** | I don't know |
| **Sai** quando parte il treno? | Do you know when the train leaves? |

Here is the present tense:

| | | | |
|---|---|---|---|
| **so** | I know | **sappiamo** | we know |
| **sai** | you know (fam.) | **sapete** | you know |
| **sa** | he/she knows, you know | **sanno** | they know |

You also use the verb **sapere** to mean 'to know how to' or 'to be able to':

| | |
|---|---|
| **Sai** far vela? | Do you know how to sail? |
| **Sapete** giocare al calcio? | Can you play football? |

### The weather

Note that the verb **fare** is often used when talking about the weather.

| | |
|---|---|
| Che tempo **fa?** | What's the weather like? |
| **Fa** bel tempo/brutto tempo | It's nice weather/bad weather |
| **Fa** caldo/freddo | It's hot/cold |

### All and everything

'All' or 'everything' in Italian is **tutto/a:**

| | |
|---|---|
| **Tutto** bene? | Is everything all right? |
| **Tutto** a posto | Everything's in order |

Note the following expressions using **tutto** in the plural:

| | | | |
|---|---|---|---|
| **tutti** i giorni | every day | **tutti** insieme | all together |

## things to do

6.1 **Un'inchiesta.** In a survey you are asked to state what sports you play.
Can you say whether or not you can do the following sports and
games?

Sai giocare . . .

a tennis   al calcio   a rugby   a golf   a scacchi (chess)

Sai . . .

nuotare   sciare   pescare   far vela   andare a cavallo (to ride).

# 6 SPORT AND LEISURE

**6.2** Next question. What do you like doing in your spare time? Can you say whether you enjoy the following activities?
1 Uscire con gli amici
2 Fare dello sport
3 Andare al teatro, al cinema, ai concerti, ecc.
4 Visitare dei musei, delle gallerie, ecc.
5 Viaggiare all'estero (abroad)
6 Rimanere a casa, fare giardinaggio, ecc.
7 Ascoltare (listen to) la radio, guardare la televisione, ecc.

**6.3** In Florence you overhear part of a conversation between a local resident and a tourist who is asking for information. Can you work out what the tourist is asking?

Turista:        ...............................................?
Passante:    No, il museo è chiuso.
Turista:        ...............................................?
Passante:    Apre alle nove della mattina.
Turista:        ...............................................?
Passante:    Chiude alle quattordici.
Turista:        ...............................................?
Passante:    No, è chiuso il lunedì.

**6.4** Can you match the following questions and answers?
1 Cosa facciamo?                  (a) Mi piace, ma preferisco il tennis.
2 Sa nuotare il bambino?          (b) No, piove sempre.
3 Fa bel tempo in Scozia          (c) Andiamo a una partita di d'inverno?                             calcio.
4 Vuoi fare il bagno?             (d) Sì, nuota come un pesce!
5 Ti piace il golf?               (e) Perchè no? Ottima idea!

**6.5 Tempo Previsto.** What's the weather like?
1 sulle regioni centrali? **2** sulle regioni settentrionali? **3** sulle regioni meridionali?

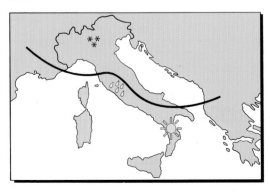

# 6 ENTERTAINMENT

## BUYING A TICKET

**Theatre, concerts**    Throughout the year there are many opera, music and drama festivals in Italy. In Venice the most important festival is the **Biennale**, while in Florence there is a big music festival, **Maggio Musicale**, in May and June. There are opera houses in Milan, Rome, Venice, Florence and Naples, and operas are also performed in many other Italian towns.

## nel ufficio prenotazioni/in the booking office

In Florence Raffaella is trying to book tickets for the opera *La Traviata*.

| | |
|---|---|
| Raffaella: | Buongiorno. **Vorrei prenotare due posti** per lo spettacolo di martedì dodici giugno. |
| Impiegato: | Mi dispiace, signora, non abbiamo più posti per quella sera. È tutto esaurito. |
| Raffaella: | Peccato! Allora, **ci sono posti per venerdì?** |
| Impiegato: | Venerdì quindici giugno. Vediamo . . . Sì, per venerdì ci sono posti in galleria e alcune poltrone. |
| Raffaella: | Quanto costano i posti in galleria? |
| Impiegato: | In galleria costano trentamila lire. |
| Raffaella: | **Mi dà due biglietti** in galleria, per favore. |
| Impiegato: | Va bene, signora. |
| Raffaella: | **A che ora incomincia** lo spettacolo? |
| Impiegato: | Alle nove. |

# 6 ENTERTAINMENT

*Booking tickets*

| | |
|---|---|
| Vorrei due biglietti per . . . | I'd like two tickets for . . . |
| lo spettacolo/il concerto | the performance/the concert |
| martedì dodici giugno | Tuesday 12th June |
| Non abbiamo più posti | We have no seats left |
| è tutto esaurito | It's completely full |
| Ci sono posti? | Are there any seats? |
| un posto in galleria/una poltrona | circle-seat/stalls-seat |
| alcune poltrone | a few seats in the stalls |
| A che ora incomincia . . .? | What time does . . . begin? |
| FERIALI/FESTIVI | WEEKDAYS/PUBLIC HOLIDAYS |

**Cinema**   Look in the entertainments page of the local newspaper or an entertainments guide to discover what's on. Films which have not been dubbed into Italian will be advertised as being in the original language (**in lingua originale**) with subtitles (**sottotitoli**).

## Il programma degli spettacoli/the entertainments page

Giancarlo and Marisa are thinking about going to the cinema, but they discover they have different tastes . . .

Marisa:    Io vorrei vedere un film. Che cosa danno?

Giancarlo: **Niente di interessante** – un western. **Non mi piacciono molto** i western.

Marisa:    Ma a me piacciono moltissimo! Come si chiama?

Giancarlo: È un film vecchio che ho già visto due volte. Si chiama *Il bello, il brutto e il cattivo*.

Marisa:    È un classico, e io non l'ho mai visto. Per favore, Giancarlo, **mi piacerebbe molto** vederlo.

Giancarlo: Va bene – andiamo. La settimana scorsa ho visto *Stregata dalla luna* con Cher che mi è piaciuto molto. In generale **mi piacciono di più** i film gialli e le commedie. Ma non importa. Facciamo i biglietti adesso e mangiamo dopo aver visto il film. **Conosco una trattoria buonissima** vicino al cinema.

*Giving your opinion*

| | |
|---|---|
| Niente di interessante | Nothing interesting |
| un film vecchio . . . | an old film . . . |
| . . . che ho già visto | . . . which I have already seen |
| due volte | twice |
| un classico | a classic |
| io non l'ho mai visto | I have never seen it |
| Mi piacerebbe molto vederlo | I'd love to see it |
| A me piace di più | I prefer |
| i film gialli | thrillers |
| le commedie | comedies |
| Regìa di . . . | Directed by . . . |
| facciamo i biglietti | we'll buy the tickets |
| mangiamo dopo aver visto il film | we'll eat after having seen the film |
| Conosco una trattoria buonissima | I know an excellent restaurant |
| INGRESSO L4000/RIDOTTO L2000 | ENTRANCE FEE/REDUCED |

# 6   ENTERTAINMENT

## the way it works

### Negatives

Look at the following phrases:

| | |
|---|---|
| **Non** abbiamo **più** posti | We have no seats left (lit. no longer) |
| **Non** vede **nessuno** | He sees nobody |
| **Non** danno **niente** d'interessante | They are showing nothing interesting |
| **Non** l'ho **mai** visto | I have never seen it |
| **Non** l'ho **ancora** fatto | I haven't done it yet |

### Before and after

'Beforehand', 'first' is **prima**. 'Before . . .' is **prima di**:

| | |
|---|---|
| Prima delle nove | Before 9 o'clock |
| Ceniamo prima di partire | We'll have supper before we go |

'Afterwards', 'later' is **dopo**. 'After . . .' is also **dopo**:

| | |
|---|---|
| Dopo le sette | After 7 o'clock |
| Ceniamo dopo aver visto il film | We'll have supper after having seen the film |

### Dates

Dates are always given in cardinal numbers (see p.78), except for the first of the month:

| | |
|---|---|
| il primo luglio | the first of July |
| il diciassette agosto | the seventeenth of August |
| il ventinove dicembre | the twenty-ninth of December |

Here are some other useful expressions with days of the week and dates:

| | |
|---|---|
| Chiuso il lunedì | Shut on Monday(s) |
| ogni sabato | every Saturday |
| venerdì trenta luglio | Friday 30th July |
| Nell' ottantanove | In 1989 |

### Future intentions

Italian often uses the present tense where English needs a future tense, to express intention or suggestion. There are some instances of this in this unit:

| | |
|---|---|
| Facciamo i biglietti | We'll buy the tickets |
| Mangiamo dopo | We'll eat afterwards |

### To know a person or a place

While **sapere** means to know *about something*, if you want to say that you know *a person or a place* you use the verb **conoscere**:

| | |
|---|---|
| Conosci Pietro? | Do you know Peter? |
| Non conosco Venezia | I don't know Venice |
| Conosco una trattoria | I know a restaurant |

64

# 6 ENTERTAINMENT

## things to do

6.6 You are at the box-office trying to buy tickets for a play.

You: [Say you want four tickets for the performance on Wednesday 19th May]

Impiegato: Mi dispiace, per mercoledì non abbiamo più posti.

You: [Ask if there are any tickets for Thursday]

Impiegato: Sì, abbiamo alcuni posti in galleria.

You: [Ask how much they are]

Impiegato: Diciassettemila lire.

You: [Say you'd like four tickets and ask how much it comes to]

6.7  1 What is being advertised here?
     2 Who is the author?
     3 Who is the director?
     4 When and at what time is it being broadcast?
     5 What is RaiDue?

**TEATRO D'ESTATE**
Paolo Stoppa
in
**IL BERRETTO A SONAGLI**
di Luigi Pirandello
**DOMANI SERA ALLE 22**
Regia di Luigi Squarzina
**RAIDUE**

     6 Can you guess what play this is?

**DA VENERDI' TUTTE LE SERE
TEATRO E CINEMA GIALLO**
Ore 20: PRIMO FILM GIALLO
Ore 21,15
*TRAPPOLA PER TOPI*
Commedia in due atti
di **AGATHA CHRISTIE**
con **ENZA GIOVINE**
*Il giallo che da 35 anni
trionfa a Londra*

6.8  1 What is being advertised?
     2 When is it on?
     3 Which day is it not open?
     4 How much does it cost?

**MUSEO D'ARTE CONTEMPORANEA
– CASTELLO DI RIVOLI:** mostra **Joan Mirò. Viaggio delle figure,** 4 giugno-18 settembre; collezione. Aperto da martedì a domenica ore 10–19, lunedì chiuso. Ingresso L. 4000, ridotto L. 2000. Per informazioni tel. 958.15.47.

# 7  SOCIAL MATTERS

## TALKING ABOUT YOUR JOB

### sono insegnante/I'm a teacher

Marisa hopes that she will be offered a job as a teacher of English and won't have to return to England. Marco is asking her about what she was doing before she came to Italy.

Marco:  Che cosa fai, Marisa?

Marisa:  **Sono insegnante. Insegnavo l'inglese** in una scuola di lingue a Londra.

Marco:  Ti piaceva abitare a Londra?

Marisa:  Abbastanza, sì. **Abitavo** in un appartamento. La mattina prendevo la metropolitana per andare a scuola – c'era una stazione a due passi dalla scuola, e **lavoravo** dalle nove alle cinque. La sera **uscivo** con gli amici . . . si andava a un *pub* . . . o al teatro, al cinema. Ci sono tante cose interessanti da fare a Londra. Mi divertivo ma . . . **volevo** sempre viaggiare, vedere il mondo.

# 7 SOCIAL MATTERS

Marco:   Dunque adesso vai a insegnare a Firenze?
Marisa:  Lo spero proprio! Domani torniamo a Firenze e spero di
         cominciare a lavorare subito.
Marco:   Mi piacerebbe imparare l'inglese. Lo vorresti insegnare
         anche a me?
Marisa:  Con piacere! Ma ti avverto, sono molto severa!

*Your work (For a list of professions see p.79)*

| | |
|---|---|
| **Sono insegnante** | I'm a teacher |
| **Insegnavo l'inglese** | I was teaching English |
| **Prendevo la metropolitana** | I went by underground |
| **per andare a scuola** | to go to the school |
| **c'era una stazione** | there was a station |
| **a due passi dalla scuola** | very close to the school |
| **Lavoravo dalle nove alle cinque** | I was working from 9 till 5 |
| **Vai a insegnare a Firenze** | You are going to teach in Florence |
| **Lo spero proprio** | I hope so very much |
| **Spero di cominciare a lavorare subito** | I'm hoping to start work at once |
| **Mi piacerebbe imparare l'inglese** | I'd like to learn English |
| **Lo vorresti insegnare anche a me?** | Would you teach me too? |
| **Con piacere!** | With pleasure |
| **Ma ti avverto, sono molto severa!** | I warn you, I'm very strict! |

*After work*

| | |
|---|---|
| **Uscivo con gli amici** | I used to go out with friends |
| **Si andava a un *pub*, al teatro** | We would go to a pub, to the theatre |
| **Mi divertivo . . .** | I was enjoying myself |
| **Ero più felice che a Roma** | I was happier than in Rome |
| **Volevo sempre viaggiare** | I always wanted to travel |
| **vedere il mondo** | to see the world |

## che lavoro fa?/what's your job?

Raffaella is stopped in the street by a reporter who asks her some questions . . .

Intervistatore:  Scusi, signora, sto facendo un'inchiesta per la RAI sugli
                 abitanti di Firenze e il loro lavoro. Vorrei farle alcune
                 domande.
Raffaella:       Con piacere.
Intervistatore:  Come si chiama, per favore?
Raffaella:       Raffaella Festoso.
Intervistatore:  **Quanti anni ha?**
Raffaella:       Trentadue.
Intervistatore:  **Di dov'è lei?** Di Firenze?
Raffaella:       No, **sono nata a Roma**.
Intervistatore:  Perché è venuta qui?
Raffaella:       Per studiare. Studiavo qui all'università di Firenze e mi
                 piaceva stare qui. Ero più felice che a Roma. Dopo gli
                 studi universitari ho trovato un posto qui.

# 7 SOCIAL MATTERS

| Intervistatore: | Che lavoro fa? |
|---|---|
| Raffaella: | **Faccio la disegnatrice** di moda. Lavoro per una ditta di tessuti. |
| Intervistatore: | È sposata? |
| Raffaella: | Sì. **Mio marito è medico**. Ci siamo incontrati dieci anni fa mentre eravamo studenti. |
| Intervistatore: | Dunque, lavorate tutti i due? |
| Raffaella: | Sì, ma io lavoro solamente la mattina. |
| Intervistatore: | Ha figli? |
| Raffaella: | Sì, abbiamo un figlio e una figlia. **Il bambino ha otto anni** e la bambina cinque. |
| Intervistatore: | Dove abitate? |
| Raffaella: | Abitiamo in un vecchio appartamento al centro. |
| Intervistatore: | Grazie. |
| Raffaella: | Prego. Buongiorno. |

| | |
|---|---|
| **Faccio la disegnatrice** | I work as a designer |
| **Lavoro per una ditta di tessuti** | I work for a fabric company |
| **È medico** | He's a doctor |
| **Faceva medicina** | He was studying medicine |
| **Lavorate tutti i due?** | Do you both work? |
| **Lavoro solamente la mattina** | I work mornings only |
| **Quanto guadagna?** | How much do you earn? |
| **Non guadagno molto** | I don't earn much |

## *Your home*

| | |
|---|---|
| **Sono nata a Roma** | I was born in Rome |
| **Sono venuta qui per studiare** | I came here to study |
| **Ci siamo incontrati dieci anni fa** | We met ten years ago |
| **mentre eravamo studenti** | when we were students |
| **Dove abitate?** | Where do you live? |
| **Abitiamo in un appartamento** | We live in a flat |
| **Abitavo in un appartamento** | I was living in a flat |
| **. . . in una casa** | . . . in a house |
| **. . . in una villetta** | . . . a small detached house |
| **le stanze, le camere** | the rooms |
| **camere da letto, bagno** | bedrooms, bathroom |
| **sala da pranzo, cucina** | dining-room, kitchen |
| **soggiorno, sala** | living-room, sitting-room |
| **giardino, terrazzo/balcone** | garden, terrace/balcony |

## *Your status*

| | |
|---|---|
| **È sposato/a** | Are you married? |
| **Sì, sono sposato/a** | Yes, I'm married |
| **fidanzato/a, vedovo/a** | engaged/widow(er) |
| **Ha figli?** | Do you have any children? |
| **Abbiamo un figlio e una figlia** | We have a son and a daughter |

# 7 SOCIAL MATTERS

## Your age

Quanti anni ha?
Trentadue
Il bambino ha otto anni
La bambina cinque

How old are you?
Thirty-two
The boy is eight
The girl five

## the way it works

### Imperfect tense

Look at the following examples from the dialogue:
Abita**vo** in un appartamento
Insegna**vo** l'inglese
**Prendevo** la metropolitana
Usci**vo** con gli amici

I was living in a flat (= used to)
I was teaching English
I took the tube (= habitual action)
I went out with friends

To talk about what you used to do or the way things used to be, you use the imperfect tense which is formed like this:
From the infinitive of the verb (e.g., **abitare, prendere, uscire**) take away the -**re** and add the following endings:

| | | | | | | | |
|---|---|---|---|---|---|---|---|
| abitare | abita | -**vo** | I lived | volere | vole | -**vamo** | we wanted |
| insegnare | insegna | -**vi** | you taught | uscire | usci | -**vate** | you went out |
| prendere | prende | -**va** | he/you took | venire | veni | -**vano** | they came |

Most verbs conform to this pattern. One exception, however is **essere**.

| | | | |
|---|---|---|---|
| **ero** | I was | **eravamo** | we were |
| **eri** | you were | **eravate** | you were |
| **era** | he/she/it was, you were | **erano** | they were |

A few other verbs use a slightly different stem: for example, **fare**.

| | | | |
|---|---|---|---|
| **facevo** | I was doing, making, etc. | **facevamo** | we were doing |
| **facevi** | you were doing | **facevate** | you were doing |
| **faceva** | he/she/it/you were doing | **facevano** | they were doing |

This tense is frequently used to express what was going on when something happened:
Ci sono incontrati mentre **eravamo** studenti. We met each other when we were students.

### Sto facendo un'inchiesta

If you want to emphasise the present time of an action you can use the present tense of **stare** (see p.11) + a form of the verb called the present participle.
The present participle is formed as follows:
-**are** verbs: remove -**are** and add -**ando**.
**sto** parl**ando**   I am talking;   **sta** pens**ando**   he is thinking
-**ere** and -**ire** verbs: remove -**ere/ire** and add -**endo**.
Cosa state fac**endo?**
Stiamo usc**endo**

What are you doing?
We are going out

# 7   SOCIAL MATTERS

## Adverbs

Adverbs are usually formed in Italian by adding **-mente** to the adjective. Adjectives which end in **-o** form their adverb from the feminine form **-a**:

lento/lenta   lentamente (slowly)   vero/vera   veramente (truly)

Adjectives ending in **-e** simply add **-mente**. But those ending in **-le** or **-re** drop the final **-e:**

facile   facilmente    difficile   difficilmente

## things to do

**7.1**   **Che lavoro fa?** Everyone is talking about what they do. Can you
answer for them? Use **Sono** . . . or **Faccio il/la** . . .

| | | | |
|---|---|---|---|
| Pietro | [doctor] | Marco | [architect] |
| Raffaella | [designer] | Paul | [company director] |
| Marisa | [teacher] | Giulia | [music student] |
| Giancarlo | [accountant] | You | (see list of jobs, p. 79) |

**7.2**   You have got into conversation with the owner of a small factory (**una azienda**) making leather goods and you are interested to know more about him:

You:       [Ask him how long he has had the factory]
Signore:   Da circa venti anni.
You:       [Ask him where he learnt to do this work]
Signore:   Da ragazzo, ho imparato qui in bottega.
You:       [You want to know how many people work here]
Signore:   Adesso nella bottega ci sono quattro persone.
You:       [Thank him very much]

**7.3**   Now it's your turn to be interviewed. The owner of the hotel where you're staying wants to know about your childhood. . .

Signora:   Di dov'è lei?
You:       [Say you were born in the South of England]
Signora:   Da ragazzo, dove abitava? In campagna o in città?
You:       [Say you lived in a village (**un paese**) in a small house, with a garden]
Signora:   Quanti eravate in famiglia? Aveva fratelli o sorelle?
You:       [Say you have a brother and a sister]
Signora:   I suoi genitori vivono ancora?
You:       [Say your mother is still alive. She is now a widow of seventy-six.]
Signora:   E suo fratello?
You:       [Say he is married with two children. He's a painter]
Signora:   E sua sorella?
You:       [Say she's not married. She's an accountant and works in London]

## A CAMPING TRIP

**Camping**    There are over 1600 campsites in Italy and camping is very popular. Tourist offices have lists of local sites and their facilities. The Touring Club Italiano publishes full details of all the authorised sites in *Campeggi e Villaggi Turistici in Italia* (TCI, Corso Italia 10, Milano). Tariffs vary according to the area and type of site.

### da quanto tempo è qui?/how long have you been here?

Back in Florence, Giulia has invited some of her friends round to meet Paul on his last evening in Italy. A friend called Franco is asking Paul about his week.

Franco:    **Da quanto tempo è qui** in Italia?
Paul:    **Da soltanto una settimana.**
Franco:    È venuto qui per lavoro o in vacanza?
Paul:    Sono venuto qui per lavoro ma sono riuscito a visitare anche Venezia, che **non avevo mai visto**.
Franco:    Allora, qual è la città che le è piaciuta di più?
Paul:    Bè . . . È difficile. Non lo so. Conosco Firenze meglio, ma tutte e due sono bellissime. Che ne pensa lei?

# 7  SOCIAL MATTERS

Franco: Io sono di Napoli e preferisco il sud di Italia – **è più** selvaggio del nord e **c'è meno** gente. Senti, Giulia, andiamo al sud per le vacanze?

Giulia: Forse. Ma ti ricordi l'anno scorso, quando siamo andati in campeggio con la tua macchina vecchia? Che disastro! (turns to Paul) Siamo andati a fare il campeggio in montagna. Prima di tutto, abbiamo avuto un guasto in autostrada. Poi, arrivati finalmente al campeggio che cercavamo, lo abbiamo trovato completo.

Franco: Sì, mi ricordo. Abbiamo trovato un altro campeggio più tardi e dopo aver messo su la tenda, avevamo fame. Ma… **avevamo dimenticato** di portare il fornello a gas…!

Giulia: Che catastrofe! Ma quest' anno hai una macchina nuova e non dimentichiamo niente!

### Small talk

| | |
|---|---|
| per lavoro/in vacanza | on business/on holiday |
| Qual è la città che…? | Which city … |
| … le è piaciuta di più? | … did you like more? |
| Conosco Firenze meglio | I know Florence better |
| Sono riuscito a visitare Venezia | I managed to visit Venice |
| Tutte e due sono bellissime | Both (cities) are lovely |
| è più selvaggio del nord | it's wilder than the north |
| c'è meno gente | there are fewer people |

### Telling a story

| | |
|---|---|
| siamo andati a fare campeggio | we went camping |
| in montagna | in the mountains |
| abbiamo avuto un guasto | we had a breakdown |
| arrivati al campeggio | when we arrived at the campsite |
| … che cercavamo | … which we were looking for |
| lo abbiamo trovato completo | we found it was full |
| dopo aver messo su la tenda | after having put up the tent |
| avevamo fame | we were hungry |
| avevamo dimenticato di … | we had forgotten to |
| portare il fornello a gas | to bring the gas cooker |

### Camping language

| | |
|---|---|
| C'è un campeggio qui vicino? | Is there a campsite near here? |
| C'è posto per una tenda/una roulotte? | Is there room for a tent/caravan |
| l'acqua potabile/la luce | drinking-water/electricity |
| una piscina/dei negozi | swimming-pool/shops |
| Dove sono i gabinetti/le docce? | Where are the toilets/showers? |

# 7  SOCIAL MATTERS

*USEFUL WORDS AND PHRASES*

| | |
|---|---|
| Non dimentichiamo niente! | We won't forget anything! |
| Che disastro!/Che catastrofe! | How awful! |
| Forse | Perhaps |

## SAYING GOODBYE

## grazie e arrivederci/thank you and goodbye

At the end of the evening Paul is saying his farewells.

Giulia: **Prendi un'altra birra?**

Paul: **No, grazie, basta così. Me ne devo andare. Parto domani mattina** presto e non ho ancora fatto la valigia. Devo essere all'aeroporto di Pisa alle dieci.

Giulia: Che peccato! **Quando ritorni** a Firenze?

Paul: L'anno prossimo, spero – in primavera. Mi auguro che tutto vada bene con gli esami. Dopo le vacanze **perchè non vieni in Inghilterra?**

Giulia: Buona idea! **Mi puoi dare il tuo indirizzo?**

Paul: Certo . . . Eccolo. Allora, grazie e arrivederci.

Giulia: Arrivederci.

73

# 7 SOCIAL MATTERS

### The end of the party

| | |
|---|---|
| Prendi un'altra birra? | Have another beer? |
| No, grazie, basta così | No, thanks, I've had enough |
| Me ne devo andare | I must go |
| Parto domani presto | I'm leaving tomorrow early |
| Non ho ancora fatto la valigia | I haven't yet packed my suitcase |
| Devo essere all'aeroporto | I must be at the airport |
| l'anno prossimo in primavera | next year in the spring |
| Quando ritorni? | When are you coming back? |
| Mi auguro che tutto vada bene | I hope all goes well |
| con gli esami | with the exams |
| Perchè non vieni in Inghilterra? | Why don't you come to England? |
| Mi puoi dare il tuo indirizzo? | Can you give me your address? |

## the way it works

### More or less

'More' is **più**. 'More . . . than' is **più . . . che** or **di**. 'Less' or 'fewer' is **meno**.

| | |
|---|---|
| Ero **più** felice **che** a Roma | I was happier than in Rome |
| . . . è **più** selvaggio **del** nord | . . . it's wilder than the north |
| C'è **meno** gente | There are fewer people |

Note that **di più** means 'most':
Quale le è piaciuto **di più**?       Which did you like most?

Note: although **più** and **meno** can be used with most comparatives, there are some which require more specialised words:

| | | | |
|---|---|---|---|
| buono (good) | **migliore** (better) | male (bad) **peggiore** (worse) (adjective) |
| bene (good) | **meglio** (better) | male (bad) **peggio** (worse) (adverb) |

### Imperfect of avere

| | |
|---|---|
| **avevo** una sorella | I had a sister |
| **avevamo** fame | we were hungry |

The formation of the imperfect of **avere** is as follows:

| | | | |
|---|---|---|---|
| **avevo** | I had | **avevamo** | we had |
| **avevi** | you had | **avevate** | you had |
| **aveva** | he/she had, you had | **avevano** | they had |

### Pluperfect tense

To say what you had done or describe what had happened, you need to use the pluperfect tense. This is formed with the *imperfect* tense of **avere** (or **essere** if the verb takes **essere** in the perfect) + the past participle:

| | |
|---|---|
| . . . che non **avevo** mai visto | . . . which I hadn't seen before. |
| . . . **avevamo** dimenticato di . . . | . . . we had forgotten to . . . |

# 7 SOCIAL MATTERS

## things to do

**7.4** Bigger and better! The children are making comparisons – to their advantage, naturally! (NB Revise possessives on p.5.)
1 La mia casa è molto grande!        [But mine is bigger than yours]
2 La mia macchina è nuova . . .
3 . . . È anche molto veloce.
4 Mio fratello è alto.
5 I nostri gelati sono buonissimi!

**7.5** **Accidenti!** Bother! It's not your lucky day. Can you say what went wrong?
1 When you arrived at the cathedral you found it was shut.
2 After having put up the tent you wanted to go to bed (**andare a letto**) but you found you had forgotten your sleeping-bag (**il sacco a pelo**).
3 You looked for (**cercare** = to look for) your suitcase but you had left it in the train.
4 You arrived at the station but the train had already gone.

**7.6** You are chatting with the owner of a local café who is interested in you and your family.

Amico: Perche è venuto qui . . . in vacanza o per lavoro?
You: [Say you came on holiday for a week]
Amico: È venuto da solo?
You: [No, say you came with your wife and daughter]
Amico: Quanti anni ha la bambina?
You: [She's ten]
Amico: Dove siete andati?
You: [Say you went camping in Tuscany]
Amico: Vi è piaciuta, la Toscana?
You: [Yes, say you liked it very much, there are some lovely old towns and the countryside (**la campagna**) is fabulous]
Amico: Siete andati a Siena?
You: [Say yes, you stopped off there for lunch one day. There is a lot to see – it's very interesting. Ask him if he knows it]
Amico: Sì molto bene. Sono nato lì – è il mio paese nativo.
You: [It's very beautiful]
Amico: Faceva bel tempo, vero?
You: [Yes, it was hot and sunny every day until yesterday (**fino a ieri**) when there was a storm]
Amico: E dove andate adesso?
You: [Say unfortunately you have to go home tomorrow. You have to be at the airport by midday]

# ANSWER KEY

**1.1** 1 Buongiorno, signore. 2 Buongiorno, signora. 3 Ciao, Claudia. 4 Buonasera, signori. 5 Ciao, Mauro.

**1.2** 1 (Mi chiamo) Henry Jones. / Sì, sono Susan Jones. 2 (Mi chiamo) Patricia Fòx./ Si chiama Ben.

**1.3** 1 (c). 2 (a). 3(d). 4(e). 5(b).

**1.4** 1 una doppia con bagno. 2 una singola con bagno. 3 una singola con doccia. 4 una doppia con due letti. 5 una singola con vista sul mare. 6 due camere singole con bagno.

**1.5** 1 Sono le tre. 2 Sono le tre e cinque. 3 Sono le tre e venti. 4 Sono le tre meno quarto. 5 È l'una.

**1.6** Due birre/ Tre bicchieri di vino rosso/ Un tè al limone/ Un caffè.

**2.1** 1 Dov'è la Piazza della Repubblica, per favore? 2 Dov'è il Palazzo Vecchio? 3 Dov'è il Palazzo Pitti? 4 Dov'è l'Azienda di Turismo? 5 Dov'è la Posta, per favore?

**2.2** 1 Il Palazzo Vecchio. 2 La Posta. 3 La Piazza della Repubblica. 4 L'Azienda di Turismo.

**2.3** 1 (c). 2 (d). 3 (e). 4 (b). 5 (a).

**2.4** Vorrei un vestito rosso; vorrei una gonna verde; vorrei dei pantaloni blu.

**2.5** 1 Mi piace quest'anello. Quanto costa? 2 Mi piace questo profumo. Quanto costa? 3 Mi piace questa spilla. Quanto costa? 4 Mi piacciono queste cinture. Quanto costano?

**2.6** . . . un paio di . . ./ Numero trentanove/ non mi piace il colore/ Posso provarli?/ Sono troppo stretti/Sì grazie/ Questi . . ./. . . buongiorno.

**3.1** del pane casereccio; delle mele e pere; dell'uva bianca; dei pomodori; del maiale; del prosciutto; degli spaghetti; del formaggio; dell'olio; dello zucchero.

**3.2** due etti di burro; un litro di latte; una bottiglia di vino rosso; mezzo chilo di mele rosse; un chilo e mezzo di pomodori maturi.

**3.3** quattrocento (4 postcards); novecento (2 stamps); millecinquecento (English newspaper); seimilaseicento (2 boxes chocs).

**3.4** 1 Mi porti un'altra sedia, per piacere? 2 Mi porti il sale e il pepe, per favore? 3 Avete pollo arrosto? 4 Avete patate fritte?

**3.5** Siamo tre. Ha un tavolo?/ Sì, va bene/ Per la signora: per primo una zuppa di pesce e di secondo una cotoletta al marsala. Per il signore: per primo delle tagliatelle alle vongole e di secondo una bistecca alla griglia. A me porti dei cannelloni al forno e di secondo prendo i pètti di pollo./ Ci può portare degli zucchini e dei funghi, per piacere./ Potremmo avere una bottiglia di Orvieto, per piacere.

**4.1** Buongiorno. Vorrei cambiare cinquanta sterline, per favore./ Sì, eccolo. Quant'è il cambio della sterlina?/ No, mi dà due biglietti da cinquantamila, per favore.

**4.2** A che ora parte il prossimo treno per Milano?/A che ora arriva?/È diretto o devo cambiare?/ Quanto costa il biglietto?/ Andata e ritorno.

**4.3** *Bologna:* il treno parte alle nove e quindici e arriva alle undici e quarantacinque. *Torino:* Parte alle dieci e venti e arriva alle dodici e cinquanta. *Firenze:* Parte alle undici e trenta e arriva alle quindici e trenta. *Ancona:* Parte alle dodici e due e arriva alle diciotto. *Roma:* Parte alle tredici e quaranta e arriva alle ventuno e trenta.

**4.4** Carla va in Inghilterra. Va in aereo./ Leo va in Francia. Va in macchina./ Antonio va a Napoli. Va in treno./ Giulia va a Orvieto. Va in pullman.

**4.5** A che ora parte il prossimo pullman per Milano?/Quanto tempo ci mette?/ Quanto costa il biglietto?/Andata./Va bene. Mi dà una andata, per favore.

**4.6** 1 Prenda la prima strada al destra. È sulla sinistra. 2 Vada fino al semaforo e attraversi la strada. È proprio lì, sulla destra. 3 Deve prendere l'autobus. Ci mette circa un'ora. La fermata è in Piazza della Repubblica.

# ANSWER KEY

**5.1** (1) Vorrei la benzina senza piombo, p.f. (2) Mi dà trenta litri, p.f. (3) Mi può controllare l'olio, p.f. (4) Mi può controllare la pressione delle gomme, p.f.

**5.2** 1 No Entry. 2 No Parking. 3 No Overtaking.

**5.3** Mi dispiace. Credo di aver lasciato la mia macchina fotografica qui/ L'ho messa sulla tavola in fondo. Ho comprato una bibita e poi ho dimenticato di prenderla./ Ah sì, questa è la mia. Grazie mille, signora.

**5.4** 1 Ho mal di stomaco. 2 Mi fanno male i piedi. 3 Ho mal di testa. 4 Mi fa male la schiena. 5 Ho mal di denti.

**5.5** Non mi sento bene. Ho vomitato e ho mal di stomaco. 2 Quante volte al giorno devo prendere le compresse? 3 Mia figlia è caduta e si è fatta male al ginocchio. Ha una benda elastica? 4 Mio figlio è stato punto. Ha qualcosa per le punture d'insetto? 5 Anche vorrei dei cerotti e della crema solare.

**5.6** 1 C'è stato un incidente. Un ragazzo si ha fatto male. Chiami un medico presto! 2 Mi è stato rubato il passaporto. L'ho lasciato ieri nella camera dell' hotel ma oggi non c'è più. 3 Una signora si è sentita male nella strada. Chiami un'ambulanza! 4 Ho perso la mia borsa. Credo di averla lasciata nel treno.

**6.1** So (Non so) giocare a tennis, giocare a calcio, giocare a rugby, giocare a golf, giocare a scacchi. So (Non so) nuotare, sciare, pescare, far vela, andare a cavallo.

**6.2** Mi piace/ Non mi piace . . .

**6.3** Il museo è aperto?/ A che ora apre?/ A che ora chiude?/ È aperto tutti i giorni?

**6.4** 1 (c). 2 (d). 3 (b). 4 (e). 5 (a).

**6.5** 1 Piove. Fa brutto tempo. 2 Nevica. Fa freddo. 3 C'è il sole. Fa molto caldo.

**6.6** Vorrei quattro biglietti per lo spettacolo di mercoledì diciannove maggio./ Ci sono posti per giovedì?/ Quanto costano?/ Allora quattro biglietti, per favore.

**6.7** 1 A play. 2 Luigi Pirandello. 3 Luigi Squarzina. 4 Sunday evening at 10 pm. 5 Channel 2. 6 *The Mousetrap*.

**6.8** 1 An exhibition of works by Mirò 2 4 June to 18 September. 3 Monday. 4 4,000 lire (reduced price 2,000 lire).

**7.1** Sono medico; disegnatrice; ragioniere; architetto; direttore; studente di musica.

**7.2** Da quanto tempo ha questa azienda?/ Dove ha imparato a fare questo lavoro?/ Quante persone lavorano qui?/ Molte grazie.

**7.3** Sono nato/a nel sud dell' Inghilterra./ Abitavamo in una villetta, una villetta con giardino, in un paese./ Ho un fratello e una sorella./ Mia madre vive ancora. È vedova e ha settantasei anni./ Mio fratello è sposato e ha due bambini. È pittore./ Mia sorella non è sposata. Lavora a Londra - è ragioniera.

**7.4** 1 La mia è più grande! 2 La mia è più nova. 3 Anche è più veloce. 4 Mio fratello è più alto. 5 I nostri gelati sono migliori.

**7.5** 1 Arrivato al duomo, lo avevo trovato chiuso. 2 Dopo aver messo la tenda volevo andare a letto, ma avevo dimenticato di portare il sacco a pelo. 3 Ho cercato la mia valigia, ma l'avevo lasciata nel treno. 4 Sono arrivato alla stazione ma il treno era partito.

**7.6** Sono venuto qui in vacanza./ No, sono con mia moglie e mia figlia./ Ha dieci anni./ Siamo andati in campeggio in Toscana./ Sì, ci è piaciuta molto la Toscana. Ci sono delle vecchie città bellissime e la campagna è favolosa./ Sì, ci siamo fermati un giorno per pranzare. C'è tanto da vedere – molte cose interessanti. La conosce lei?/ È bellissima./ Sì, faceva bel tempo tutti i giorni fino a ieri. Ieri c'era una tempesta./ Purtroppo domani dobbiamo andare a casa. Dobbiamo essere all' aeroporto a mezzogiorno.

# TOPIC VOCABULARIES

## English–Italian topic vocabularies

### Numbers 0–100

| | | | | | | | |
|---|---|---|---|---|---|---|---|
| 0 | zero | 11 | undici | 21 | ventuno | 40 | quaranta |
| 1 | uno | 12 | dodici | 22 | ventidue | 50 | cinquanta |
| 2 | due | 13 | tredici | 23 | ventitrè | 60 | sessanta |
| 3 | tre | 14 | quattordici | 24 | ventiquattro | 70 | settanta |
| 4 | quattro | 15 | quindici | 25 | venticinque | 80 | ottanta |
| 5 | cinque | 16 | sedici | 26 | ventisei | 90 | novanta |
| 6 | sei | 17 | diciassette | 27 | ventisette | 100 | cento |
| 7 | sette | 18 | diciotto | 28 | ventotto | | |
| 8 | otto | 19 | diciannove | 29 | ventinove | | |
| 9 | nove | 20 | venti | 30 | trenta | | |
| 10 | dieci | | | | | | |

### Numbers 101–100 000

| | | | |
|---|---|---|---|
| 101 | centouno | 2 000 | duemila |
| 102 | centodue | 3 000 | tremila |
| 110 | cento dieci | 4 000 | quattromila |
| 200 | duecento | 5 000 | cinquemila |
| 300 | trecento | 6 000 | seimila |
| 400 | quattrocento | | |
| 500 | cinquecento | 10 000 | diecimila |
| 600 | seicento | 20 000 | ventimila |
| 700 | settecento | 50 000 | cinquantamila |
| 800 | ottocento | 100 000 | centomila |
| 900 | novecento | 500 000 | cinquecentomila |
| 1000 | mille | 1000 000 | un milione |

### Ordinal numbers

| | |
|---|---|
| first | primo/a |
| second | secondo/a |
| third | terzo/a |
| fourth | quarto/a |
| fifth | quinto/a |
| sixth | sesto/a |
| seventh | settimo/a |
| eighth | ottavo/a |
| ninth | nono/a |
| tenth | decimo/a |

### Months

| | |
|---|---|
| January | gennaio |
| February | febbraio |
| March | marzo |
| April | aprile |
| May | maggio |
| June | giugno |
| July | luglio |
| August | agosto |
| September | settembre |
| October | ottobre |
| November | novembre |
| December | dicembre |

# TOPIC VOCABULARIES

## Days of the week

| | |
|---|---|
| Monday | **lunedì** |
| Tuesday | **martedì** |
| Wednesday | **mercoledì** |
| Thursday | **giovedì** |
| Friday | **venerdì** |
| Saturday | **sabato** |
| Sunday | **domenica** |
| week | **la settimana** |
| weekend | **il finesettimana** |
| next week | **la prossima settimana** |

## Times of the day, etc.

| | |
|---|---|
| morning | **la mattina** |
| afternoon | **il pomeriggio** |
| evening | **la sera** |
| night | **la notte** |
| today | **oggi** |
| this morning | **stamattina** |
| tomorrow | **domani** |
| tomorrow morning | **domani mattina** |
| yesterday | **ieri** |
| last week | **la settimana scorsa** |

## Professions

| | |
|---|---|
| accountant | **ragioniere, ragioniera** |
| architect | **architetto** |
| businessman | **uomo d'affari** |
| civil servant | **funzionario/a** |
| clerk | **impiegato/a** |
| computer operator | **operatore** |
| computer programmer | **programmatore** |
| dentist | **dentista** |
| designer | **disegnatore, disegnatrice** |
| doctor | **medico** |
| engineer | **ingegnere** |
| electrician | **elettricista** |
| estate agent | **agente immobiliare** |
| journalist | **giornalista** |
| lawyer | **avvocato, avvocatessa** |
| manager, director | **direttore** |
| nurse | **infermiere/a** |
| mechanic | **meccanico** |
| painter | **pittore** |
| pensioner | **pensionato/a** |
| potter | **ceramista** |
| policeman | **poliziotto** |
| retired | **in pensione** |
| salesman | **rappresentante** |
| secretary | **segretaria** |
| shop assistant | **commesso/a** |
| student | **studente** |
| teacher | **insegnante, maestro/a** |
| technician | **tecnico** |
| unemployed | **disoccupato/a** |
| worker | **operaio** |

## Clothes (l'abbigliamento), etc.

| | |
|---|---|
| women's/men's | **per donna/uomo** |
| children's | **per bambini** |
| anorak | **la giacca a vento** |
| bathing costume | **il costume da bagno** |
| bikini | **il bikini** |
| blouse | **la camicetta** |
| bra | **il reggiseno** |
| briefs | **lo slip** |
| coat | **il cappotto** |
| dress | **il vestito** |
| gloves | **i guanti** |
| handbag | **la borsa** |
| handkerchief | **il fazzoletto** |
| hat | **il cappello** |
| jacket | **la giacca** |
| jeans | **i jeans** |
| jersey | **la maglia** |
| pullover | **il pullover** |
| raincoat | **l'impermeabile** |
| scarf | **la sciarpa** |
| shirt | **la camicia** |
| shorts | **i pantaloncini** |
| skirt | **la gonna** |
| socks | **i calzini** |
| suit (man's) | **il completo** |
| suit (woman's) | **il tailleur** |
| sweater | **il maglione** |
| swimming costume | **il costume da bagno** |
| swimming trunks | **i calzoncini da bagno** |
| tee-shirt | **la maglietta di cotone** |
| tie | **la cravatta** |
| tights | **il collant** |
| tracksuit | **la tuta sportiva** |
| trousers | **i pantaloni** |
| tweed jacket and trousers | **uno spezzato** |

# TOPIC VOCABULARIES

## Shoes

| | |
|---|---|
| shoes | le scarpe |
| boots | gli stivali |
| clogs | gli zoccoli |
| sandals | i sandali |

## Colours

| | |
|---|---|
| black | nero/a |
| blue | blu, azzurro/a |
| brown | marrone |
| green | verde |
| grey | grigio/a |
| orange | arancione |
| pink | rosa |
| purple | viola |
| red | rosso/a |
| white | bianco/a |
| yellow | giallo/a |
| light . . . | . . . chiaro/a |
| dark . . . | . . . scuro/a |

## Shops (i negozi) and services (i servizi)

| | |
|---|---|
| bank | la banca |
| barber's | il barbiere |
| bookshop | la libreria |
| camping equipment | il materiale da campeggio |
| chemist's | la farmacia |
| clothes shop | l'abbigliamento |
| dry-cleaner's | la lavanderia a secco |
| hairdresser's | il parrucchiere |
| hardware store | il negozio di ferramenta |
| jeweller's | la gioielleria |
| launderette | la lavanderia automatica |
| library | la biblioteca |
| newsagent | il giornalaio |
| police-station | la questura |
| post-office | la posta |
| shoe-shop | il negozio di scarpe |
| souvenirs | il negozio di oggetti ricordo |
| sporting goods | il negozio di articoli sportivi |
| stationer's | la cartoleria |
| tobacconist's | la tabaccheria, il tabaccaio |
| toyshop | il negozio di giocattoli |
| travel-agency | l'agenzia di viaggi |

## At the chemist's

| | |
|---|---|
| antibiotic | l'antibiotico |
| antiseptic cream | la crema antisettica |
| aspirins | le aspirine |
| bandage | la garza, la benda |
| cotton wool | l'ovatta |
| cough-pastilles | le pasticche per la tosse |
| eye-drops | le gocce per gli occhi |
| laxative | il lassativo |
| medicine | la medicina |
| pills | le compresse |
| plasters | i cerotti |
| prescription | la ricetta |
| sleeping-pills | i sonniferi |
| tablets | le pastiglie |

## Toiletries and other items

| | |
|---|---|
| aftershave | la lozione dopobarba |
| babyfoods | gli alimenti per bebè |
| brush | la spazzola |
| comb | il pettine |
| contact-lens liquid | il liquido per lenti a contatto |
| contraceptives | gli anticoncezionali |
| cream | la crema |
| deodorant | il deodorante |
| disposable nappies | i pannolini |
| perfume | il profumo |
| razor | il rasoio |
| razor-blades | le lamette |
| safety-pins | le spille di sicurezza |
| sanitary-towels | gli assorbenti igienici |
| shampoo | lo shampoo |
| shaving-cream | la crema da barba |
| soap | il sapone |
| sunglasses | gli occhiali da sole |
| suntan lotion | la crema solare |
| talc | il talco |
| tampons | i tamponi igienici |
| tissues | i fazzolettini di carta |
| toothbrush | lo spazzolino da denti |
| toothpaste | il dentifricio |

# TOPIC VOCABULARIES

## Food

### Fruit (la frutta)

| | |
|---|---|
| apple | la mela |
| apricot | l'albicocca |
| banana | la banana |
| cherry | la ciliegia |
| grapes | l'uva |
| fig | il fico |
| lemon | il limone |
| lime | il cedro |
| melon | il melone |
| orange | l'arancia |
| peach | la pesca |
| pear | la pera |
| plum | la susina |
| pineapple | l'ananas |
| raspberries | i lamponi |
| strawberries | le fragole |
| walnuts | le noci |
| watermelon | l'anguria |

### Vegetables (la verdura)

| | |
|---|---|
| artichoke | il carciofo |
| asparagus | gli asparagi |
| beans | i fagioli |
| French beans | i fagiolini |
| cabbage | il cavolo |
| carrot | la carota |
| cauliflower | il cavolfiore |
| cucumber | il cetriolo |
| chicory | l'indivia |
| courgettes | gli zucchini |
| garlic | l'aglio |
| lettuce | l'insalata |
| leek | il porro |
| mushrooms | i funghi |
| olives | le olive |
| onion | la cipolla |
| parsley | il prezzemolo |
| peas | i piselli |
| pepper | il peperone |
| potato | la patata |
| spinach | gli spinaci |
| tomato | il pomodoro |

### Meat (la carne) and poultry (il pollame)

| | |
|---|---|
| beef | il manzo |
| kidneys | i rognoni |
| lamb | l'agnello |
| lamb cutlet | cotoletta d'agnello |
| liver | il fegato |
| pork | il maiale |
| pork chops | braciole di maiale |
| steak | la bistecca |
| veal | il vitello |
| veal escalope | scaloppina di vitello |
| chicken | il pollo |
| chicken breasts | petti di pollo |
| duck | l'anatra |

### Fish (i pesci) and shellfish (frutti di mare)

| | |
|---|---|
| anchovies | le acciughe |
| bass | il branzino |
| clams | le vongole |
| cod | il merluzzo |
| cuttlefish | la seppia |
| eel | l'anguilla |
| lobster | l'aragosta |
| mackerel | lo sgombro |
| mussels | le cozze |
| octopus | il polpo |
| oyster | l'ostrica |
| prawns | i gamberoni |
| red mullet | la triglia |
| sardines | le sardine |
| salmon | il salmone |
| squid | i calamari |
| trout | la trota |
| tuna | il tonno |

## Parts of the body (il corpo)

| | |
|---|---|
| ankle | la caviglia |
| arm | il braccio |
| back | la schiena |
| blood | il sangue |
| bone | l'osso |
| chest | il torace |
| ear | l'orecchio |
| eye | l'occhio |
| face | il viso |
| finger | il dito |
| foot | il piede |
| hair | i capelli |
| hand | la mano |
| head | la testa |
| heart | il cuore |
| knee | il ginocchio |
| leg | la gamba |
| lung | il polmone |
| mouth | la bocca |

# TOPIC VOCABULARIES

| | | | |
|---|---|---|---|
| muscle | il muscolo | deck-chair | una sedia a sdraio |
| nose | il naso | fishing-tackle | degli arnesi da pesca |
| rib | la costola | pedal-boat | un moscone |
| shoulder | la spalla | rowing-boat | una barca a remi |
| skin | la pelle | sailing-boat | una barca a vela |
| stomach | lo stomaco | sailboard | un surf, tavola a vela |
| throat | la gola | water-skis | degli sci nautici |
| tooth | il dente | skis | degli sci |
| toe | il dito del piede | ski-boots | degli scarponi da sci |
| | | ski-sticks | dei bastoncini |
| | | skates | dei pattini |

## Parts of the car (la macchina)

| | | | |
|---|---|---|---|
| battery | la batteria | game | il gioco |
| brakes | i freni | match | la partita |
| carburettor | il carburatore | golf-course | il campo da golf |
| clutch | la frizione | ski-run, piste | la pista |
| engine | il motore | swimming-pool | la piscina |
| exhaust | il tubo di scappamento | tennis-court | il campo da tennis |
| fan-belt | la cinghia del ventilatore | | |

## Places to visit and natural features

| | |
|---|---|
| headlights | i fari |
| ignition | lo spinterogeno |
| indicator | l'indicatore |
| plugs | le candele |
| tyre | la gomma |
| wheel | la ruota |
| windscreen | il parabrezza |

| | |
|---|---|
| art gallery | la galleria d'arte |
| bridge | il ponte |
| building | l'edificio |
| castle | il castello |
| cathedral | il duomo |
| chapel | la cappella |
| church | la chiesa |
| concert-hall | la sala dei concerti |
| exhibition | la mostra |
| fountain | la fontana |
| gardens | i giardini |
| island | l'isola |
| lake | il lago |
| market | il mercato |
| monastery | il monastero |
| monument | il monumento |
| museum | il museo |
| palace | il palazzo |
| park | il parco |
| river | il fiume |
| ruins | le rovine |
| square | la piazza |
| stadium | lo stadio |
| statue | la statua |
| theatre | il teatro |
| tower | la torre |
| town-hall | il municipio |
| university | l'università |

## Sports and games

| | |
|---|---|
| athletics | l'atletica |
| basketball | il pallacanestro |
| chess | gli scacchi |
| climbing | l'alpinismo |
| cycling | il ciclismo |
| fishing | la pesca |
| football | il calcio |
| golf | il golf |
| racing (car) | la corsa automobilistica |
| racing (horse) | la corsa di cavalli |
| sailing | la vela |
| skiing | lo sci |
| swimming | il nuoto |
| tennis | il tennis |
| volleyball | la pallavolo |

### Sports equipment

| | |
|---|---|
| I'd like to hire | Vorrei noleggiare . . . |
| racket | una racchetta |
| bathing hut | una cabina |

# VOCABULARY

## Italian–English Vocabulary

**a** at, in, to
**abbastanza** quite, fairly
**abitante** *m.* inhabitant, resident
**accanto a** beside
**accettare** to accept
**accomodarsi** to make oneself comfortable; **s'accomodi** please do, go ahead, do sit down
**accompagnare** to accompany
**accordo: d'accordo** agreed, I agree
**aceto** *m.* vinegar
**acqua** *f.* water; **– minerale** mineral water
**adesso** now
**aereo** *m.* aeroplane
**aeroporto** *m.* airport
**agenzia** (*f*) **di viaggi** travel agency
**aggiungere** to add
**agnello** *m.* lamb
**agosto** August
**aiuto** *m.* **help**
**al, all', allo, alla, etc.** at the, in the, to the
**albergo** *m.* hotel (plural **alberghi**)
**alimentari** *m.pl.* groceries
**allora** well then, now
**alto/a** tall, high; **– pressione** high pressure
**altro/a** other; **vuole altro?** do you want anything else? **senz'altro** of course
**alzarsi** to get up
**ambasciata** *f.* embassy
**ambulanza** *f.* ambulance
**americano/a** American
**amica** (*f*), **amico** (*m*). friend
**anche** too, also; **anch'io** me too
**ancora** yet
**andata** *f.* single (ticket); **– e ritorno** return (ticket)
**andare** to go, drive; **andiamo** let's go; **– a letto** to go to bed
**anello** *m.* ring
**anno** *m.* year
**antipasto** *m.* starter (course)
**aperto/a** open
**appartamento** *m.* appartment, flat
**appuntamento** *m.* appointment
**apribottiglia** *m.* bottle-opener
**aprile** April
**aprire** to open
**arancia** *f.* orange
**aria condizionata** *f.* air-conditioning
**arrivare** to arrive

**arriverderci, arrivederla** goodbye
**arrivo** *m.* arrival
**arrosto** roasted
**articolo** *m.* article
**ascensore** *m.* lift
**ascoltare** to listen to
**aspettare** to wait
**assicurazione** *f.* insurance
**assortiti** assorted
**attenzione!** careful!
**attimo** *m.* moment
**attravesare** to cross
**augurare** to wish
**autonoleggio** *m.* car rental
**automobile** *f.* car
**automobilista** *m/f.* motorist
**autostrada** *f.* motorway
**autunno** *m.* Autumn
**avere** to have; **aver bisogno** to need
**avvertire** to warn
**avvocato** *m.* lawyer
**azienda** *f.* factory, firm; **– di soggiorno e turismo** tourist information office

**bagaglio** *m.* luggage
**bagno** *m.* bath, swim
**balcone** *m.* balcony
**bambina** *f.* girl
**bambino** *m.* child, boy
**banca** *f.* bank
**bar** *m.* bar, café
**barbiere** *m.* barber's
**barca** *f.* boat
**basso/a** low; **bassa pressione** low pressure
**bastare** to be enough; **basta!** enough! **basta così** that's all
**beh…** well…
**bel, bello/a** lovely, beautiful, nice
**bene** fine, good well; **ben cotto/a** well-cooked (steak); **ben arrivato/a!** welcome! **va bene** fine, OK; **benissimo** excellent, great
**benzina** *f.* petrol
**bere** to drink
**bevanda** *f.* (soft) drink, beverage
**bianco/a** white
**bibita** *f.* (soft) drink
**bicchiere** *m.* glass
**bicicletta** *f.* bicycle
**biglietteria** *f.* ticket window, counter
**biglietto** *m.* ticket note; **– da visita** business card

# VOCABULARY

binario *m.* platform
birra *f.* beer
bisogno: aver – to need
bistecca *f.* steak
bitter *m.* type of aperitif
blu blue
bocca *f.* mouth
borsa *f.* handbag
bottega *f.* workshop
bottiglia *f.* bottle
braccio *m.* arm
braciola *f.* chop; – di maiale pork chop
brindisi *m.* toast
brutto bad
buca (*f*) delle lettere letter-box
buonanotte good night
buonasera good evening
buongiorno good morning
buono/a good
burro *m.* butter

cabina (*f*) telefonica telephone box
cadere to fall
cacciatore: alla – cooked in sauce
    containing onions, tomatoes,
    mushrooms, peppers, wine
caffè *m.* coffee, cafeteria
caffelatte *m.* white coffee
calcio *m.* football
caldo hot
calmo calm
cambio *m.* exchange, rate of exchange
camera *f.* room, bedroom
cameriera *f.* waitress
cameriere *m.* waiter
camicia *f.* shirt
campanile *m.* bell-tower
campeggio *m.* campsite, camping
campo *m.* field; – da tennis tennis-court
capire to understand
cappello *m.* hat
carabinieri *m.pl.* police
caraffa *f.* jug
carne *f.* meat
caro/a expensive
carta *f.* paper; – di credito credit-card;
    – stradale map; – verde green card
    (car insurance); – d'identità identity
    card
cartolina *f.* postcard
casa *f.* house, home
casereccio/a homemade (bread etc)
caso *m.* case
cassa *f.* cash-desk

castello *m.* castle
cavallo *m* horse; andare a – to ride
cena *f.* dinner
cenare to have dinner
centralinista *m/f.* telephone operator
centro *m.* centre
ceramista *m.* potter
cercare to look for
cerotto *m.* plaster
certo certainly
che? what?
chiamare to call; to telephone
chiamarsi to be called
chiave *f.* key
chiesa *f.* church
chilo *m.* kilo
chilometro *m.* kilometre
chiudere to close
chiuso/a closed
chiusura *f.* closing
ci here, there; c'è there is; ci sono
    there are
ciao! hello! goodbye!
cielo *m.* sky
cinema *m.* cinema
cintura *f.* belt
circa about
città *f.* town, city
cognome *m.* surname
coincidenza *f.* connection
colazione *f.* breakfast
colore *m.* colour
coltello *m.* knife
come as, like, how; come? how? what?
cominciare to begin
comodo/a comfortable
compilare to fill in (form)
completo/a full
comprare to buy
compressa *f.* pill
compreso/a included
con with
concerto *m.* concert
conoscere to know (person or place)
consigliare to advise
conto *m.* bill, account
contorno *m.* vegetable (with main dish
    in restaurant)
controllare to check
controllo (*m*). passaporti passport
    control
contusione *f.* bruise
coperto *m.* cover charge; overcast
    (sky)

# VOCABULARY

corriera *f.* coach, country bus
corso *m.* avenue
cosa *f.* thing; che cosa? cosa? what?
così like this, thus; così così so so
costare to cost
cotoletta *f.* cutlet; – alla milanese
    dipped in egg and breadcrumbs,
    then fried
cotone *m.* cotton
credo I think
crudo raw; prosciutto – smoked ham
cucchiaio *m.* spoon
cucina *f.* kitchen

da at, by, for, from, of
dal, dall', dallo, dalla, etc. at the, by the,
    for the, from the, of the
dare to give
davanti in front
davvero? really?
del, dell', dello, della, etc. of the, some,
    any
denaro *m.* money
dente *m.* tooth
dentista *m/f.* dentist
dentro inside
denuncia *f.* report
desiderare to want; desidera?
    desiderano? what would you like?
dessert *m.* sweet, pudding
destinazione *f.* destination
destra *f.* right; a – to/on the right; sulla –
    on the right
deve (see dovere)
deviazione *f.* diversion
dicembre December
dichiarare to declare
dietro behind
dimenticare, dimenticarsi to forget
dire to say, tell
diretto direct; *m.* stopping train
direttore *m.* director, manager
direzione *f.* direction, management
diritto straight on
discoteca *f.* discotheque
disegnatrice *f.* designer
dispiace: mi – I'm sorry
disponibile available
ditta *f.* firm, company
divertirsi to enjoy oneself
doccia *f.* shower
documento *m.* document
dogana *f.* customs
dolce *m.* sweet, pudding

domanda *f.* question
domani tomorrow
domenica Sunday
domicilio *m.* place of residence
donna *f.* lady
dopo after
dopodomani the day after tomorrow
doppio/a double
dormire to sleep
dove? where? dov'è? where is?
dovere to have to; deve prendere il
    treno you must take the train
dritto straight on
dunque well, so
duomo *m.* cathedral

e and
è (see essere)
ecco here is
edificio *m.* building
elenco (*m*) telefonico telephone
    directory
entrare to enter
entrata *f.* entrance
errore *m.* mistake
esame *m.* exam
esattamente exactly
esaurito sold out
espresso *m.* fast train
essere to be
est *m.* east
estate *f.* Summer; d'– in the Summer
estero: all'– abroad
etto *m.* 100 grams

facchino *m.* porter
famiglia *f.* family
fare to do, make; – il biglietto to buy
    one's ticket; una settimana fa a week
    ago
farmacia *f.* chemist
favoloso/a fabulous, great
favore: per – please
febbraio February
febbre *f.* fever, temperature
fegato *m.* liver
felice happy
fermarsi to stop
fermata *f.* bus-stop
ferroviaria: la stazione – railway station
fetta *f.* slice
fidanzata *f.* fiancée; fidanzato fiancé
figlia *f.* daughter
figlio *m.* son

# VOCABULARY

**fiammiferi** *m.pl.* matches
**fine** *f.* end
**finesettimana** *m.* weekend
**finestra** *f.* window
**finire** to finish
**fino a** as far as, until
**Firenze** Florence
**firma** *f.* signature
**firmare** to sign
**fondo: in** – at/to the end, bottom, back
**fontana** *f.* fountain
**forchetta** *f.* fork
**formaggio** *m.* cheese
**fornello** (*m*) **a gas** gas-cooker
**forno** *m.* oven; **al** — baked
**forse** perhaps
**forte** strong
**fotografare** to photograph
**fragola** *f.* strawberry
**francese** French
**Francia** France
**francobollo** *m.* stamp
**fratello** *m.* brother
**freddo/a** cold
**frittata** *f.* omelette
**fritto/a** fried; **– misto** dish of mixed fried
   fish
**fronte: di** – opposite; **di – a** in front of
**frullato** *m.* milkshake
**frutta** *f.* fruit; **frutti di mare** shellfish
**fruttivendolo** *m.* greengrocer
**fumatori** *m.pl.* smokers
**fungo** *m.* mushroom; **i funghi**
   mushrooms
**funzionare** to work (of machines)
**furto** *m.* robbery
**fuori** outside

**gabinetto** *m.* toilet
**galleria** *f.* art gallery; circle (theatre)
**Galles** Wales
**gallese** Welsh
**gamba** *f.* leg
**garage** *m.* garage
**gasolio** *m.* diesel
**gassato/a** fizzy, carbonated
**gelateria** *f.* ice-cream parlour
**gelato** *m.* ice-cream
**gente** *f.* people
**genitore** *m.* parent
**gennaio** January
**gentile** kind
**gettone** *m.* telephone token
**ghiacciato/a** frozen

**ghiaccio** *m.* ice
**già** already
**giacca** *f.* jacket
**giallo/a** yellow
**giardino** *m.* garden
**giocare** to play
**gioco** *m.* game, play
**giornale** *m.* newspaper
**giornata** *f.* day
**giorno** *m* day
**giovane** *m.* young man
**giovedì** Thursday
**girare** to turn; **giri** turn
**giro** *m.* tour
**gita** *f.* trip
**giugno** June
**gli** the (m.pl.); to him
**gola** *f.* throat
**gomma** *f.* tyre
**gondola** *f.* gondola
**gonna** *f.* skirt
**grado** *m.* degree
**grammo** *m.* gram
**Gran Bretagna** Great Britain
**grande** big
**grave** serious
**grazie** thank you; **– mille** many thanks
**grigio/a** grey
**griglia: alla** – grilled
**guadagnare** to earn
**guardare** to watch, look at
**guasto** *m.* breakdown
**guidare** to guide

**ho, hai, ha, hanno** (see **avere**)
**hotel** *m.* hotel

**i** the (m.pl)
**ieri** yesterday
**il** the (m. sing)
**imparare** to learn
**importa: non** – it doesn't matter
**in** in, to
**incassare** to cash
**inchiesta** *f.* survey
**incidente** *m.* accident
**incominciare** to begin
**incrocio** *m.* crossroads
**indigestione** *f.* indigestion
**indirizzo** *m.* address
**informazione** *f.* information
**Inghilterra** England
**inglese** English
**ingresso** *m.* entrance

# VOCABULARY

insalata *f.* salad
insegnante *m/f.* teacher
insegnare to teach
insieme together
isola *f.* island
Italia Italy
italiano/a Italian

la the (f.sing.); you, her, it
lago *m.* lake
lana *f.* wool
largo/a wide (plural **larghi/e**)
lasciare to leave
latte *f.* milk
latteria *f.* dairy
lavarsi to wash (oneself)
lavorare to work
lavoro *m.* work, job
le the (f.pl); to/for you
lei you (sing.); she; her
lentamente slowly
lento/a slow
letto *m.* bed
li them
lì there; **lì in fondo** down there
libero/a free
libreria *f.* bookshop
lieto: molto – nice to meet you
limonata *f.* lemonade
limone *m.* lemon
linea *f.* line; **resti in** – hold the line
lingua *f.* language
lira *f.* lira (unit of currency)
litro *m.* litre
lo the (m. sing); him, it
Londra London
lontano/a far
loro their
luglio July
lui he, him
lunedì Monday
lungo/a long (plural **lunghi/e**)

ma but
macchina *f.* car, machine; – **fotografica** camera
macellaio, macelleria *f.* butcher's
madre *f.* mother
maggio May
maggiore eldest, major
maglione *m.* sweater
magro/a lean (meat)
mai never
maiale *m.* pork

mal: – **di testa** headache; – **di stomaco** stomach-ache; – **di denti** toothache
malato/a ill, sick
male bad, badly; **non c'è male** not bad; **fa** – to hurt
mamma *f.* mummy
mancia *f.* tip
mandare to send
mangiare to eat
mano *f.* hand (plural **le mani**)
manzo *m.* beef
mare *m.* sea
marito *m.* husband
marrone brown
martedì Tuesday
marzo March
matrimoniale: **camera** – room with double bed
mattina *f.* morning
meccanico *m.* mechanic
medico *m.* doctor
meglio better
mela *f.* apple
meno less; – **un quarto** quarter to (time)
menù *m.* menu
mercato *m.* market
mercoledì Wednesday
mese *m.* month
messaggio *m.* message
metro *m.* metre
metropolitana *f.* underground (railway)
mettere to put
mezzanotte midnight
mezzo/a half; – **pensione** half-board; **mezz'ora** half an hour
mezzogiorno midday
mi me; to/for me; myself
migliore better
milanese: **alla** – dipped in egg and breadcrumbs and fried
mille thousand
minestra *f.* soup
mio, mia, etc. my, mine
misto/a mixed
moda *f.* fashion
modello *m.* model, type
moderno/a modern
modo *m.* way, manner
moglie *f.* wife
molto a lot (of), many; very (much)
mondo *m.* world
monte *m.* mountain
montagna *f.* mountain(s)
monumento *m.* monument

# VOCABULARY

morire to die
mortadella *f.* type of sausage
mostra *f.* exhibition
mostrare to show
motocicletta *f.* motorbike
mozzarella *f.* type of cheese
museo *m.* museum
musica *f.* music

nascere to be born
Natale Christmas
nazionalità *f.* nationality
ne some (of it/of them)
nebbia *f.* fog
negoziante *m.* shopkeeper
negozio *m.* shop
nel, nell', nello, nella, etc. in the
nero/a black
nessun, nessuno/a no, none; nobody
neve *f.* snow
niente nothing
no no
noleggiare to hire
noleggio *m.* rental, hire
nome *m.* name
non not
nonna *f.* grandmother
nord *m.* north; **nord-ovest** north-west
normale normal; 2-star (petrol)
nostro/a our
notte *f.* night
novembre November
nulla anything, nothing
numero *m.* number; size (shoe); –
  **sbagliato** wrong number; – **di
  immatricolazione** registration
  number
nuotare to swim
nuoto *m.* swimming
nuovo/a new
nuvola *f.* cloud
nuvoloso cloudy

o or
occhiali *m.pl.* glasses; – **da sole**
  sunglasses
occupato/a occupied
offerta *f.* offer
oggi today
ogni every
olio *m.* oil
oliva *f.* olive
ombra *f.* shade
ombrellone *m.* beach umbrella

opera *f.* opera, work
oppure or else
ora *f.* time, hour; – **di pranzo** lunchtime
orario *m.* timetable; – **di visita** opening
  hours
orecchio *m.* ear
orologio *m.* clock, watch
ospedale *m.* hospital
ostello (*m*) della gioventù youth-hostel
ottimo/a excellent, great
ottobre October
ovest west

pacchetto *m.* packet
padre *m.* father
paese *m.* village, country
pagare to pay
paio *m.* pair
palazzo *m.* palace
pane *m.* bread
panetteria *f.* baker's
panino *m.* bread-roll
panna *f.* cream
pantaloni *m.pl.* trousers
parcheggiare to park
parcheggio *m.* car-park, parking
parlare to speak
parrucchiere *m.* hairdresser's
parte *f.* part: a – separately
partenza *f.* departure
partire to depart, leave
partita (*f*) di calcio football match
passaggio: di – en route, on the way
passante *m.* passer-by
passaporto *m.* passport
passare to spend; pass; – **per** to go
  along
passo *m.* step; **a due passi** very close
  (two steps)
pasticceria *f.* sweet and cake shop
pasto *m.* meal
patata *f.* potato
patente *f.* driving-licence
pattini *m.pl.* skates; – **a rotelle** roller
  skates
peccato: che peccato! what a pity!
pecorino *m.* sheep's milk cheese
pedaggio *m.* toll charge
peggio worse
pelle *f.* leather
pellicola *f.* film (roll)
penna *f.* pen
pensione (*f*) completa full board
pepe *m.* pepper

# VOCABULARY

**per** for
**pera** *f.* pear
**perchè** because, why?
**perdere** to lose
**pericoloso** dangerous
**permesso** allowed
**pescare** to fish
**pesce** *m.* fish
**pescheria** *f.* fishmonger's
**piacere** to please; **mi piace** I like (it); **mi piacciono** I like (them)
**piacere** *m.* pleasure; pleased to meet you; **per** – please
**piano** *m.* floor, storey; **pianterreno** ground floor
**pianta** *f.* town map
**piatto** *m.* plate, dish
**piazza** *f.* square
**piccante** strong (flavoured)
**piccolo/a** small
**piede** *m.* foot: **a piedi** on foot, walking
**pieno/a** full; **fare il pieno** to fill up (with petrol)
**pila** *f.* battery
**pioggia** *f.* rain
**piombo** *m.* lead
**piovere** to rain
**piscina** *f.* swimming pool
**più** more, most; **più che** more than; **di più** most of all; **in più** over and above **non . . . più** not any more, no longer
**po':** **un po' di** a little (bit) of
**poco:** **un poco** a little
**poi** then
**polizia** *f.* police
**pollo** *m.* chicken
**poltrone** *f.pl.* stalls (theatre)
**pomeriggio** *m.* afternoon
**pomodoro** *m.* tomato
**ponte** *m.* bridge
**portabagagli** *m.* boot (of car); porter
**portafoglio** *m.* wallet
**portare** to bring, carry, take
**possibile** possible
**posso** I can (see **potere**)
**posta** *f.* post-office
**posto** *m.* seat; job
**potere** to be able
**pranzare** to have lunch
**pranzo** *m.* lunch
**preferire** to prefer
**prefisso** *m.* area code
**prego** not at all, don't mention it

**prego?** what would you like?
**prelevare** to withdraw (cash)
**prendere** to take; to catch (train, etc); to have (drink, etc)
**prenotare** to book
**prenotazione** *f.* booking, reservation
**preoccuparsi** to be worried
**prescrivere** to prescribe
**presentare** to present
**pressione** *f.* pressure
**presto** early, soon
**preventivo** *m.* estimate
**previsioni del tempo** weather forecast
**previsto/a** expected
**prezzo** *m.* price
**primavera** *f.* Spring
**primo/a** first; **per primo** as a first course; **la prima colazione** breakfast
**profumo** *m.* perfume
**pronto** ready; hello! (on telephone); – **soccorso** first aid
**proprio** really, just; – **qui** just here
**prosciutto** *m.* ham
**prossimo/a** next
**provare** to try, to try on
**provenienza** *f.* origin, starting from
**pullman** *m.* coach
**punto/a** stung (from **pungere** to sting)
**puntura** *f.* sting; – **d'insetto** insect bite
**pure:** **entri** – come in, of course

**quadro** *m.* painting, picture
**qualcosa** something
**quando?** when?
**quanto?** how much?; **quant'è?** how much is it? **quanti/e?** how many?
**quarto** *m.* quarter
**quel, quell', quello, quella** that; **quei, quegli, quelle** those
**questo/a** this; **questi/e** these
**qui** here

**raffreddore** *m.* cold
**ragazza** *f.* girl; **ragazzo** *m.* boy
**rallentare** to slow down
**rapido** *m.* fast inter-city express train
**respirare** to breathe
**retro:** **vista sul** – gives onto the back (of building)
**ricetta** *f.* prescription
**ricevimento** *m.* reception
**ricevuta** *f.* receipt
**ricordarsi** to remember
**riduzione** *f.* reduction

# VOCABULARY

rimanere to stay, remain
rimettere to put back
riparare to repair
riscaldamento *m.* heating
riservare to reserve
ristorante *m.* restaurant
ritardo *m.* delay; in – late
ritornare to return
ritorno: andata e – return ticket
riuscire to succeed
rivista *f.* magazine
rosso/a red
roulotte *f.* caravan
rovescio *m.* shower (of rain)
rubare to steal; mi è stato rubato . . . my
  . . . has been stolen

sabato Saturday
sacchetto *m.* carrier-bag
sala *f.* room; – da pranzo dining-room
salame *m.* salami sausage
sale *m.* salt
salumeria *f.* delicatessen, grocer's
salsa *f.* sauce
saltimbocca alla romana dish
  consisting of slices of ham and veal
  fried in butter then braised in white
  wine
sandali *m.pl.* sandals
sangue: al – rare (steak)
sapere to know
sbagliare to make a mistake
sbagliato mistaken, wrong
scacchi *m.pl.* chess
scarpe *f.pl.* shoes
scatola *f.* box, tin
scheda *f.* form
scegliere to choose
scendere to get off (bus, etc.)
sci *m.* skiing
sciare to ski
scontrino *m.* receipt
scorso/a last; la settimana – last week
Scozia *f.* Scotland
scozzese Scottish
scuola *f.* school
scusi! excuse me! I beg your pardon!
se if
secolo *m.* century
secondo/a second; di – for second
  course
sedia *f.* seat, chair
selvaggio/a wild
semaforo *m.* traffic-lights

sempre always
senso unico one way street
senta! senti! listen!
sentirsi to feel
senza without; senz'altro of course
sera *f.* evening
servire to serve
servizio *m.* service
seta *f.* silk
settembre September
settimana *f.* week
si one, you; yourself, oneself, himself,
  herself, themselves
sì yes
sicuro/a sure
sigaretta *f.* cigarette
signora *f.* lady, Mrs
signor(e) *m.* gentleman, Mr
signorina *f.* young lady, Miss
singolo/a single
sinistra *f.* left; a – to/on the left; sulla –
  on the left
so I know (see sapere); non lo so I don't
  know
soggiorno *m.* living-room
soldi *m.pl.* money
sole *m.* sun
solo only, alone
soltanto only
sono I am; they are (see essere); ci
  sono there are
sorella *f.* sister
spazioso/a spacious, large
sperare to hope
spesa *f.* shopping
spesso often
spettacolo *m.* performance
spiaggia *f.* beach
spiccioli *m.pl.* small change
spilla *f.* brooch
spingere to push
sport *m.* sport
sposarsi to get married
sposato/a married
spremuta *f.* fresh fruit juice
stagione *f.* season
stamattina this morning
stanco/a tired
stanza *f.* room
stare to be (well, etc); come sta? how
  are you?
stasera this evening.
stato/a been (past. part. of essere)
stazione *f.* station; – ferroviaria railway-

# VOCABULARY

station; – **di servizio** service station
**sterlina** *f.* pound sterling
**stesso/a** same; **lo** – the same (thing)
**strada** *f.* street
**stradale** (of the) street
**stravagante** odd, strange
**stretto/a** narrow, tight
**studente** *m.* student
**studiare** to study
**su** on, up
**subito** at once, right away
**succo** *m.* juice
**sud** *m.* south
**sugo** *m.* sauce
**sul, sull', sullo, sulla, etc.** on the
**suo, sua, etc.** your, his, her, its
**super** four-star (petrol)
**supermercato** *m.* supermarket
**supplemento** *m.* surcharge
**surf** *m.* sailboard
**surriscaldare** to overheat

**tabaccheria** *f.* tobacconist's
**tabaccaio** *m.* tobacconist
**taglia** *f.* size (clothes)
**taglio** *m.* cutting
**tanto/a** so much, very much, a lot
**tardi** late
**tariffa** *f.* fare
**tassì** *m.* taxi
**tavola, tavolo** table
**tazza** *f.* cup
**te** you
**tè** *m.* tea
**teatro** *m.* theatre
**tedesco/a** German
**telefonata** *f.* telephone call
**tempo** *m.* time, weather
**temporale** *m.* thunderstorm
**tenda** *f.* tent
**tenero/a** tender
**terrazza** *f.* terrace
**testa** *f.* head
**ti** you; to/for you
**tirare** to pull
**toilette** *f.* toilet, lavatory
**torace** *m.* chest
**tornare** to return
**torta** *f.* cake, gateau
**tosse** *f.* cough
**tovagliolo** *m.* table napkin
**traghetto** *m.* ferry
**trattoria** *f.* restaurant
**treno** *m.* train

**troppo** too (much)
**trovare** to find
**trovarsi** to be (situated)
**tu** you (sing)
**tuo, tua, etc.** your, yours
**turismo** *m.* tourism
**turista** *m/f.* tourist
**tutto** all, everything; – **a posto** everything in order; **tutto/a** every, all **tutti e due** both

**ufficio** *m.* office
**ultimo/a** last
**un, un', uno, una** a, an, one
**università** *f.* university
**uomo** *m.* man
**uovo** *m.* egg (plural *f.* **uova**)
**usare** to use
**uscire** to go out
**uscita** *f.* exit
**uva** *f.* grape(s)

**va** (see **andare**); **va bene** OK, fine
**vacanza** *f.* holiday
**vada!** go!
**vado** I'm going (see **andare**)
**valigia** *f.* suitcase
**vaniglia** *f.* vanilla
**vaporetto** *m.* motorboat
**vecchio/a** old
**vedere** to see
**vedova** *f.* widow
**vela: far** – to sail
**veloce** fast
**vendere** to sell
**venerdì** Friday
**venire** to come
**vento** *m.* wind
**verde** green
**verdura** *f.* vegetable
**vermut** *m.* vermouth
**vero?** isn't it? aren't you? etc
**verso** about
**vestito** *m.* dress
**vetrina** *f.* shop-window
**vettura** (*f*) **ristorante** restaurant-car
**vi** to/for you; yourselves; there
**via** *f.* street
**viaggiare** to travel
**viaggio** *m.* trip, journey
**viale** *m.* avenue
**vicino/a** near
**vietato/a** prohibited
**villetta** *f.* small detached house

# VOCABULARY

**vino** *m.* wine
**visitare** to visit
**vista** *f.* view
**vita** *f.* life
**vitello** *m.* veal
**voi** you (plural)
**volere** to want
**volo** *m.* flight
**volta** *f.* time; **qualche volta** sometimes

**vomitare** to be sick, vomit
**vorrei** I'd like (see **volere**)
**vostro/a** your
**vuole** (see **volere**)

**zoccoli** *m.pl.* clogs
**zucchero** *m.* sugar
**zucchini** *m.pl.* courgettes
**zuppa** *f.* soup